AGAPE love is Cure

Talicia Parker

AGAPE love is Cure

Edited by Lisa Thompson at www.writebylisa.com.
You can email Lisa at writebylisa@gmail.com for your editing needs. Thank you, Lisa, for your time, patience, encouragement and perseverance in editing this book.

Formatted by Rik - Wild Seas Formatting (www.WildSeasFormatting.com)

All scriptures in this book are taken from the King James Version (KJV). Public Domain, except Psalms 124:1-3, which was taken from the NIV.

Warning of sensitive content:

This book contains stories of sexual abuse, and the contents are intended for mature readers.

Paperback ISBN: 13-978-1-7323792-0-6

Table of Contents

Introduction

I would be remiss not to give God the credit for this book. Because of God, I am still here, alive, well, and in my right state of mind. Psalm 124:1-3 tells us, "If the LORD had not been on our side - let Israel say - when people attacked us, they would have swallowed us alive when their anger flared against us;" If the Lord had not been at my side, where would I be? Had it not been for God who kept me safe and in my right mind, I would have just lost it. If anyone knows hurt, I do. If anyone knows deep disappointment, I do. If anyone knows failure, neglect, abuse, rejection, and betrayal, I do.

And if anyone knows what it's like to love unconditionally and in spite of all these negative things, I do. I'm writing this book under the authority of the Holy Spirit because those negative experiences have taught me so much. Therefore, I know that as you continue to read this book, you will experience breakthrough after breakthrough in every area of your life. This book is designed to empower both believers and non-believers. No matter who you are, no matter where you live, no matter what you had to pass through, you can understand that everyone needs love. I know this book will bless you because it is written to the glory of God.

This book is designed to shed light on why giving and receiving love is so important. Love also helps us to evolve into the perfect being, which is God's idea of love. This book will also impart information as to why the desire of the enemy is to wipe love out of the hearts and minds of mankind. It is also a tool to help you guard your hearts with all diligence, for out of it flow the issues of life. (See Proverbs 4:23.) When the thief comes, you will not allow him to rob you of your love, which is connected to your joy and your peace.

I know that this book is written by the inspiration of the Holy Spirit, who teaches all things and leads and guides us into all truth. Because I have been through so many negative personal experiences that would have wiped out the average person, I know there is power in love because I still stand, and I still have made a decision to love. As I'm writing the pages of this book, I'm asking the Holy Spirit why he laid this topic on my heart—me of all people. With tears rolling down my cheeks, I still type as the Holy Spirit answers me. "Because despite the hell you've endured, you refuse to allow the enemy to wipe out the love of God in your heart for mankind."

One day after a long review of my miserable life, I had to ask, "God, is this hell? Are we living in hell on earth? This has to be hell. If not, then why do I feel so tormented? Why am I suffering with so much agony and pain? Because either this is hell, or you don't love me at all." You might have asked these same questions a time or two in your life. I was so tired; I just needed a moment of peace. Please. I couldn't find peace anywhere. And I surely couldn't trust anyone.

I assure you that the answers that you find in these pages will awaken you and heighten your awareness of God's love. I will help you discover the reasons why things happened to you. Together, we will uncover truths that will take you to a new level of understanding.

From the beginning of time, mankind has or will experience pain of some sort—be it hurt, disappointment, betrayal, being lied to, being a victim of abuse, neglect, or perhaps even as an abuser. But the issue here is why? Why is there so much calamity? In today's society, there's pain wherever you turn. From a worldwide lack of water to a personal lack of support, problems abound. From wars to rumors of wars, there is calamity. One can't help but ask the question *why*? And where is God in all this?

Remember that although we experience pain, hurt, starvation, terror, or any other problems, God is not the author of this pain, for he is not the author of confusion but of peace (1 Corinthians 14:33).

Distractions

While you read this book, remember that I speak from a place of authenticity, a place of experiences learned from God. The material that I'm sharing with you here has been revealed to me through experiences, dreams, and revelational knowledge from God. Please know and understand that, yes, God still speaks to us. In many cases, I had a dream and woke up from the dream asking questions about what the dream meant. Later on in life, I began to have experiences that my dreams had the answers to. My dreams have pointed out answers to many of life's daily problems. My friend, please keep this in mind while reading. I tell you this so that you might find answers to many of life's issues through my experiences as well. You will hopefully apply the principles that I've learned along with the Word of God to help guide you through any tough times or challenges that you or a loved one might face so, that should adversity arise you will not become distracted by the tactics of the enemy, but you will remember that his goal is to rob you of your right to love.

Chapter One:
How It All Started:
The Day I Heard God Say,
"Write a Book on Love"

You should have seen the puzzled look on my face the day God put this book in my heart. I was like an owl, "Who, me?" Of course, this came after I'd reluctantly accepted a full duty call to ministry. I felt like I needed to have a discussion with God. I said, "Now wait a minute, God. First of all, I don't even feel qualified for ministry; now you want me to write a book about love? No, I'm the last person on earth who should even speak on love. Weren't you there, Lord, during all those years of my pain, hurt, rejection, betrayal, and molestation at the hands of those you placed in charge of me?" My mind couldn't help but replay the beginning days of my earlier years. I continued, "Lord, look. I don't want to replay this in my mind anymore."

Suddenly, I flashed back to age three. My dad placed me on the bathroom toilet with the seat down and began to fondle me. I was just lying there, staring at him with a filthy look on my face. He moved me across the hall from our bathroom to the bedroom. There I was with my hero on top of me as he pleasured himself. I didn't know what was happening, but I knew it wasn't right. As I stared deep into his eyes, he seemed to understood my wordless plea because he couldn't stand the sight of my painful, piercing eyes staring at him, silently screaming, "No, Daddy, no! This is wrong!" The screams of my eyes shining through from my soul to his must have been unbearable. He covered my face with a pillow so that he didn't have to look at me.

One day, he came to pick me up on a bicycle with the yellow child seat attached to the back. What bittersweet times! I was happy to see him yet sad, too young to understand it all. I didn't know whether to smile due to happiness at seeing my dad and spending time with him or if I should scream because a monster seemed to be living inside of him. The monster came out sometimes, and I didn't know what was going on because I was so young. The very thought of this weakened me to my core. Isn't it something how those who were supposed to love us violated us? But it's okay today because I am free. I don't write this book from a place of hurt; no, this story is told from a place of victory, not defeat.

In addition, others sexually violated me as well, which created wedges in the family. My mom finally got away from the relationship with my dad. I was so relieved because of their unhealthy and strange relationship. Somehow, they always seemed to put me in the middle of their arguments. I was a child and should not have to choose between them.

Now momma was in a new relationship. In the beginning, I was really happy about mom's new-found love. But sadly, this guy acted just like my dad. In fact, he was just the same, just a little bit smoother and sneakier. One day, I returned home from a weekend trip only to find this guy moving around in the middle of the night, trying to fill and feed his sick addiction. I finally let momma know that he was touching one of my siblings. It was sure a weight off my shoulders because I didn't want to break her heart with the truth that he was actually sexually involved with me. Instead, I just told her about my sibling.

When I broke the news to her, she was confused. She didn't seem to understand what I was saying. I thought that I would validate and prove my point further in hopes that she would receive the truth and remove all doubt. I thought that I should go ahead and tell her that he was touching me too. Well, that idea didn't work out too well. Even after I told her, he was still around. This really made me feel badly. I wanted to ask, "Mom, do you actually believe this man cares about you when all of the signs that he doesn't are clearly there? He doesn't help you. All you do is argue about the most basic things, and on top of that, he's sexually active with your children."

At this point, I told my pastor that I was leaving when I turned fourteen unless she got rid of this man because he was no good. It was a shame that I felt that I couldn't tell the pastor everything that was going on. But my parents warned me not to talk about these types of things to outsiders. My brothers and sisters and I were almost taken into foster care when I was eight years old. I felt such horrible pressure as a child in that situation. The abuse and dysfunction in our home had become so bad that I planned to leave home at fourteen, and I did just that. I thought, *If I'm going to be fondled, I might as well choose who is fondling me.* I started dating older men, just trying to figure out a way to get out of that house. I met a man who was about twenty-three years old. I had him ask my mom if he could marry me. I was so foolish. Surprisingly, my mom told him yes. Looking back, I still can't believe it. Of course, that relationship didn't work out. In fact, I wasn't even a virgin although he was my first boyfriend. I don't remember losing my virginity. I thought there was supposed to be a bloody show. Where was mine? I guess because of the sexual violations, somewhere along the way, my virginity was stolen. I have no idea when that happened. It might have been before I could even remember.

At fourteen years old, I decided, "You know what; I will just go and live with my grandma. Truth is, I'd rather be anywhere than here in this house. I despise men that put their filthy hands on children." So off to Granny's house I went. But the only problem was that my dad was there, and he was a known rapist. But I was older now. I thought, *Surely, he wouldn't dare to try and touch me. I can defend myself now. I can say no.* About a week went by at Granny's; all was well. I felt comfortable and happy. On this particular night, I asked my cousins why they were arguing about who would sleep on the outside of the bed and why they were so afraid in their own house.

They stared at me, looking stuck and at a loss for words. I told them, "I will sleep on the outside again tonight. You guys have nothing to fear." In the middle of the night, we were all sound asleep. But someone came to the side of the bed and began fondling my private parts. It was dark, and I couldn't see. I wasn't very spiritual knowledgeable about spiritual matters, but I thought that this looked like something demonic, so I punched this thing and chased away whatever it was from the side of the bed. This man looked like a creature crawling around on all fours. I went to the kitchen for a knife, not to kill anyone but to place inside the door. I was thinking, *Oh no, that was my dad. He's still doing the same things.* I had never seen anything like that before. It appeared as if this man had gotten worse. So I locked the door with the knife. I sat there until I began to doze off to sleep again.

I woke up again. This time, he came in the room through the basement. I had forgotten to block that entrance. I really didn't think it was necessary, but I was wrong. Here he came again, this time through the basement door that led up to the bedroom. I fought him off and screamed at him to leave us alone. I went to the kitchen for four more knives, two for the room door and two for the basement door. This was the craziest thing I'd ever seen. I looked at my cousins who were there in the room with me, terrified. They had been dealing with this every night. No wonder they fought to sleep near the wall. Whoever was on the outside of the bed would be molested. So finally, I said to them, "Don't worry. It's okay. You guys can rest now. I have secured the doors; he cannot get in anymore." I sat up all night—shocked, hurt, embarrassed, and confused, totally at a loss for words. I couldn't believe that this just happened. My grandma was old. I didn't want to bother her with such foolishness.

I sat there puzzled until I drifted off to sleep for the third time. I once again woke to the sound of the window opening. This time, he was trying to climb through the bedroom window. I couldn't believe it! I couldn't see his face clearly, but I started cracking him with a broomstick that I brought from the kitchen. Now we had to get a stick to lock the window, or we wouldn't be able to sleep in peace.

This is what my life was like. And here I am now still standing, after spending years getting delivered. God told me, "Yes, and that's why I selected you for the job of writing about my love. Because you overcame all of that."

I answered, "No, Lord, I don't think I qualify. You know how misunderstood I am."

He again said, "Yes, it's okay to be misunderstood and viewed as a fool for a while, but you must tell them. Not only did you make it out, but you remained with your love intact. Tell them how I had to walk you through the season when I commanded you to love them anyway."

I understand that people didn't do right by you the way that they should have. My message to you is that—in spite of your pain, anger, and frustration, in spite of the fact that those you were depending on let you down, that those who were designed to protect you hurt you, in spite of all of that—God still require us to love them. I know it's a lot to swallow. I said, "God, are you kidding me? You still expect me to love those people after all the hell they put me through? They were so wrong, and you still want me to love them? You must want me to be taken for some type of fool!"

But then I heard a small voice say, "In order to make it, you will have to be looked at as a fool for a little while."

I said, "What?" Yes, did you not know that God intentionally places the righteous among the wicked? Yes, he does. The purpose for that is to create game changers. Yes, my friend, some of you have been handpicked and selected to be agents of change. Don't twist around what I'm saying. I'm in no way saying that God has selected you to go through the pain, but he has graced you with the ability to do so without being broken. In fact as a result, you will be stronger after you experienced pain. That's why the Bible teaches that what the enemy meant for your evil, God will make for your good. (See Genesis 50:20 and Romans 8:28.)

I honestly don't quite know why, out of all the people on earth, God chose Talicia Parker to write on the subject of love. You should have seen my face when the idea of a book on love crossed my mind, and God placed it in my spirit. I thought, *Who, me? Please. No, it can't be me. I am not the love poster child. After all I suffered from abuse at the hands of those who were responsible for loving me and they didn't, I should be disqualified.*

I told the Lord, "You need a picture-perfect girl for this one." I'm writing so much of what I thought, you see, so apparently the Lord wasn't listening to me. He did, however, inform me that I had endured the pain and had experienced the hardship and lack of love but was still able to resist the enemy and take a stand against the devil. I informed him that he can't have my love. Yes, I told the enemy that he would not wipe love from my life. See, I found out something as I begin to look down the corridors of my life. I noticed the enemy always working through someone, causing them to commit an offense against another, to make them angry or distant. The purpose is to create a snowball effect. A snowball effect begins small and if not put to an end, it will continue to roll and build until it's no longer a snowball but a massive destructive force on the move with speed and height and weight and depth.

I grew up in the inner city of Chicago, the West Side. When I was a teen, we moved to a housing project, and life for me was rough ever since I could remember. At times, I asked God, "Do you hate me? What have I done to deserve all this pain? Why did you place me in this family? Is this hell?" I even took the time to look up the definition of hell. Life for me as a youth was so tough that I thought that I was living a life of hell.

I found this: "a place regarded in various religions as a spiritual realm of evil and suffering, often traditionally depicted as a place of perpetual fire beneath the earth where the wicked are punished after death."[1] After reading this definition and comparing and contrasting it with my life, I said to myself, "Surely, I must be dead. I feel like I'm in hell already."

I was brought up in my neighborhood not to tell people all of our business, let alone to go to counseling. The reason for that was linked to fear. You know the story. As the saying goes, "What goes on in this house stays in this house," meaning that the last thing you ever wanted to do was to reach outside of your house for help. That meant getting the so-called ABC people involved or the Department of Children and Family Services (DCFS). This, however, only left me vulnerable and unable to handle challenges that could have been put to rest a long time ago.

This, my friend, was one of the reasons I began to drink. I drank every day, probably to cover up the pain. I couldn't believe a father would do something like that to his only daughter. I felt unloved by him and even felt unloved by my mom. And since my dad was labeled a rapist, deep down inside I took all of this to heart. So here I was at age seventeen, getting drunk every day. I lived to get drunk. It didn't take away the pain, but it helped me to not feel. I drank until I was twenty-nine years old. The first six months without drinking, I counted back and couldn't believe that I had been drinking for twelve years, a long time.

I was on this journey, and I couldn't quite understand why I drank every day. I guess I thought I needed something to calm my nerves because I was also very short on patience when I was not drinking. Sometimes I was so nice and kind yet other times in a full-blown rage. I didn't trust people at all. And I never gave people the opportunity to snake me. So I walked around hard all the time. I broke off friendships on a dime. I didn't care for men very much, and I certainly didn't want to get married. In my mind, all men were no good. At one point, I said, "Well, maybe I'm a lesbian." But then I discovered that wasn't true; I did like men after all. Yet I still didn't trust them. In fact, I didn't trust anyone but God because he wasn't a man. The truth is that the real me had been buried underneath all those bad experiences: all the hurt, lies, betrayals, and let downs. I had so many things stacked up against me and so much pain

---

[1] *Oxford Dictionaries*, "hell (*n.*)," accessed February 27, 2018, https://en.oxforddictionaries.com/definition/hell

that I was carrying. I had a good heart; I know I did, but I refused to let it out or let it show. So I walked around uncomfortable and frowning all the time because that's how I felt, but that was not who I truly was.

It's taken me years to realize that. And oh, how I longed for so many years to let my cuddly lovable self—the real me—shine through. Deep down inside, I loved people so much, but I didn't feel safe enough to allow them to see or experience that love. As a child, I learned the saying, "It's a dog-eat-dog world out here, and only the strong survive." So I decided that I would be strong, I was hard. I appeared mean. But that's just how I appeared; that wasn't who I was. I wanted to express my love to others, but when I saw the behavior of those who displayed a cold and cruel heart, I didn't trust them. So I allowed the real me to stay hidden and stay out the way. And I thank God for placing it in my heart to want to change. At the same time, I didn't quite understand how. Just like many of you, there's a vulnerable person inside of you. Like me, you really want to be yourself and let that person out.

If you have never been abused, then you don't know what it's like. The molestation that I endured from my dad was so awful and painful. He should have loved and protected me, provided for me. What a bitter pill to swallow from the man who was supposed to give to me. Instead, he took from me. I didn't even give up my virginity; it was taken from me; I don't even remember when. For years, my heart ached, longing to be loved for real. I knew that the way my family acted was not real love. While my dad molested me, he looked at me, asking, "Do you like that?" I stared back at him, not understanding fully what was happening at the time as I was only three years old. Somehow I knew that this was wrong. I stared at him while I was drinking my bottle as he was doing his thing. As I said before, that was when he finally placed a pillow over my face so that I wouldn't look in his eyes. I don't tell my story to be vindictive nor do I hold anything against my dad. He has suffered enough. Let me explain.

Around the time my dad turned fifty, I spoke to him on the phone. We had hours of catching up to do. He sounded concerned with the fact that he was growing older and worried about who would take care of him in his old age. To be quite frank with you, I'm not sure if my dad is even aware that I remember those times he molested me. I don't remember him penetrating me but rubbing his privates against mine. As I was saying, I don't believe he knows that I know. But somehow this one day in particular, he started crying to me on the phone, saying, "Talicia, I was a fool. I didn't know how to love anyone. I didn't even love myself."

In my heart, I took that as acknowledgement and an apology. I could tell this man was suffering. The Bible says that, "for of the abundance of the heart his mouth speaketh" (Luke 6:45b). He went on to say how proud he was of me. He said, "Talicia, you made it through so many rough spots. I thought you were outta there." I cannot begin to explain how liberating it was to hear him say that he was proud of me! It was like a sigh of relief, an affirmation, an apology, even though he didn't fully express that.

Once I left my mother's house, I was looking for love in all the wrong places—in the arms of men. I was looking for the love I never felt I had. All I could think of was starting a family. On the outside, I appeared hard, and yes, I was, yet I lacked something. I made up my mind that no one in this world can be trusted. I didn't want any close ties to anyone for fear that I'd only be let down again. So my relationships were cut short, and I made sure that I found a reason to leave people alone. Deep down inside, I was looking for the love I felt I never had. Yet at the same time, I desired a family. At times, I'd think, *Man, I never want to bring a child into this world to face all of these challenges. I just want to be happy. I just want to get it right.* But my response was all wrong. Seeking love caused me to connect with what society considered menaces. Though labeled a menace of society, in my personal opinion, these were ordinary human beings who either lacked love or made wrong choices during a time of crisis. After that, they coped by using the few survival skills that they knew. Alcohol and drug addiction soon followed, which brought on more poor choices.

The problem in the inner city is that we lack leadership. I'm talking about hands on leadership with which the community can connect. We need this connection in order to grasp the attention of inner city youth and parents alike. We need the sort of leadership that has not forgotten what it means to be without, what it means to have hope, dreams, and information that will cause an individual to rise from their current mind set.

By now, I was ten. I had been molested by not only my own dad but by my stepdad as well. Looking back, I'm sure my mom was too confused and emotionally tied to her men to handle the situation, which left me feeling unloved, betrayed, and rejected by her. So at fifteen, I left home out of fear, rejection, feeling neglected, abused, and ashamed of my family. I too was confused. By the time I was seventeen, I began looking for love from others, feeling as if it didn't exist with my family. I was lost and embarrassed. Family members teased me. "Your daddy is a rapist." By then, my dad had been in and out of the penal institution for rape.

But although I grew up with a poor self-image, my mom gave me a strong foundation despite her own struggles. She shared the love of God with me, which was the only thing that allowed me to hold it together. She taught us to reverence God and took us to church at least three days a week before I left home. God is the one thing that I have always held on to.

Unresolved Issues

Science tells us that every adult issue can be linked back to an unresolved childhood issue.[2] Based on my own personal experience, I believe that to be true. These unresolved issues are enough to make anyone run away from home. And if they are not dealt with, you might be running all of your life. As a fourteen-year-old girl, I ran away from home from the skillet right into the fire. I had the idea that I just wanted to start my own family. I wanted to make it big. I loved God but because I lost the honor and respect for my mother. The rift in our relationship caused me to be leery of her judgement. Sad to say, I felt that I really couldn't trust her. I love my dad dearly as well. But the decisions they made created a wedge between us.

I was a very young, beautiful girl dating drug dealers. I knew momma said it was wrong, but I FELT as though I couldn't trust her judgement. In my eyes, she didn't know what was up in the world. The enemy set up these traps in the minds of young people. The devil will take every opportunity to steal from you, rob you, and trick you. I don't blame anyone who allowed the enemy to use them; I blame the evil one. But I still hold these people accountable for allowing themselves to be deceived so that the enemy could gain a foothold in my life.

I spent time with my uncle, who was the chief of a well-known gang. I thought my uncle was cool especially because he'd never tried to hit on

---

[2] Carolyn Gregoire, "Why This Doctor Believes Addictions Start In Childhood," *Huffington Post*, January 26, 2016, https://www.huffingtonpost.com/entry/gabor-mate-addiction_us_569fd18ae4b0fca5ba76415c.

me, so I loved and respected him a great deal. He had a trap house in a huge abandoned building that I often visited. Just imagine a sixteen-year-old young lady going in and out of an abandoned twenty-unit building. No lights in the halls. Dead bodies popping up from time to time. Most of the time, I was drunk as a skunk.

By the time I was nineteen, I'd been arrested over a dozen times for anything from mob action to drugs. I was out there, ya'll. And my heart was cold. After all I'd been through, I didn't trust anyone. I even wanted to be the queen of the gang and asked my uncle about this when I was about twelve years old. I wanted to be in the gang because my uncle was a man that people respected; they were afraid to cross him. I was so excited. I asked, "So, what do I need to do?" You should have seen my face when he told me that I had to sleep with the whole gang. I became very quiet and didn't ask him again for years. When I was about seventeen, I asked him again because I thought he just said that to keep me out of the gang. But he gave me the same answer, so that fantasy came to a quick end.

Next, I decided to just date some high rollers. Everyone in the hood wants to live that ghetto fabulous lifestyle, at least I did. The lifestyle earned us respect on those streets and kept our families safe. At least for a little while. My point here is not to glorify Satan or any wrong doing; my point is to show you how easily the enemy can creep in and steal our children from us. So as a parent, you must watch and pray. Pray with your eyes open and learn to be sober minded. Don't allow a man or anyone to ruffle your feathers or throw off your mood. That's a distraction from the enemy to keep women emotionally out of balance to the point where you don't see what's going on in your house, and you miss the small telltale signs. In fact, if anyone emotionally throws your life out of balance, cut those people loose. The enemy will attack you when you are thrown off balance. One example is when a person continues to argue with you over the littlest petty thing. Situations like this cause our children to wander away from what is right and begin to walk in error.

I can truly say that I know, according to Psalm 124:1-2, "Had it not been for the Lord who was on my side, where would I be?" As a nineteen-year-old teenager, I was riding with a boyfriend and his friend. We pulled near a community building in a high-traffic drug area, and the two guys got out of the car. I felt uncomfortable in my spirit. I told my friend that

I wasn't comfortable and asked why we were there. I wanted to leave. Of course, he was on drugs, so he didn't want to listen to me at all. I heard a still, small voice say, "Get in the front seat, and when I tell you to pull out, you pull out." I looked in the ignition, and my boyfriend had left the car running. I didn't know what to do. I heard that still, small voice become stronger and speak with more authority a second time. "Get in the front seat now." I still sat there, becoming more and more uncomfortable. The voice of the Holy Spirit, that still, small voice, spoke a third time with even greater authority. "Get in the front seat *now*! Don't get out! Crawl over the front seats." This voice spoke so authoritatively that I had to move quickly.

Something serious was about to happen; I just didn't know what. After I'd moved into the front seat, I hoped this guy would come out of the building. I really didn't want to leave in his car. But I couldn't ignore the voice of the Holy Spirit speaking and warning me. So I waited until the Holy Spirit said, "Drive." Still, I waited. I heard the same thing a second time. The third time, the Holy Spirit told me, "Take off *now*!" I finally listened, glory be to God. And as soon as we made it to the corner, we saw a guy with a huge gun shoot and just miss us as we reached the corner. We drove to a friend's house nearby where we were safe. The owner of the car we were in was pistol whipped. He told us that the only reason they didn't kill him was because we had gotten away and saw one of the attackers. I said, "Thank you, Jesus."

God was at work in my life and kept me even when I didn't realize it. He kept me and protected me when I made foolish decisions. And he will do the same for you. His word says in Jeremiah 29:11, "For I know the plans I have for you says the Lord, plans to give you a future, a hope and an expected end" (paraphrase).

When I was nineteen, I obtained a job working for an insurance company, making pretty good money. At the time I lived in a housing project where they charged you according to your income. Before I started working, my rent was $40 per month. After I got this job, my rent increased to $600 per month. I said, "No, I'm not willing to pay an extra $540 monthly to remain in public housing." So I moved out and never returned. I started out in an apartment then, years later, became a first-time home buyer. Shortly after that, I decided to move to the suburbs. What a difference! In the suburbs, everyone was nice and kind and looked out for one another. This was quite a change. You could leave your personal items outside, and no one would bother them. I loved it. The longer I stayed away, the more accustomed to kindness I became. One day, I returned to Chicago to check on my property. All of a sudden, the same lady who once lived and walked fearlessly through the projects felt fear come over her. I thought, *Oh, my God, I hope no one snatches my purse.* I rushed to my car as fast as I could.

As I sat in the car, I heard a still, small voice say, "You have lost your connection to the community. Don't lose your connection." I forgot that in the hood nobody just robs you. In fact, if they can't help you, they surely won't hurt you. Even the guys who stand on the corners are just there trying to survive. In the hood, there have to be dire circumstances, such as a heavy drug abuser or kids starving, before someone just robs you or does anything to you.

My point here is that when people leave impoverished communities, we have the tendency to look down on the same people who are where we once were. The problem is that we cannot be effective when we totally disconnect from where we grew up.

I thought, *No, these are my people, and they are same as I am. I know the problems they face very well. I know the pain and worries they feel, the fate they're afraid of; I know this place all too well.* The fact of the matter is that it doesn't matter what nationality or color or gender you may be—man, woman, boy, or girl—we all face the same challenges.

From a Daughter to a Father

A bit more of my dad's story follows. When he was nearing fifty years old, we were laughing on the phone about him becoming half-a-hundred. That laughter quickly faded to a cry, and I imagined tears pouring down his face. As I listened to the sadness in his voice, he began to cry out of a broken and disappointed heart. "I was a fool. I was a fool not to love my family. I didn't love anyone, not even myself. I didn't know what love was or what it was all about. And here I am, now fifty years old. I see so much that I should have been better at, but I just didn't know how to love." I guess this was his way of apologizing. I told him that I understood.

During our phone conversations I began to dig deeper. I asked about his childhood. I learned that my grandmother was a slave. She did not know her mother and was wed at the age of thirteen. I also learned that my dad only saw his own dad twice in his life. Apparently, my dad never had a relationship with his own dad.

During these calls with my dad, I learned that he would have to spend time in an institution for repeat offenders. I asked him what it was like in there. I asked him what makes a man rape a woman. He said that they do it for the thrill, for the rush. I said, "They do? Don't they know the negative effects that will have on the victims?"

He replied, "No, they never consider the outcome, just the thrill."

I asked, "Well, what about child molesters?

He told me that, in their mind, the child likes it. Their mind tricks them. He also said that women shouldn't dress provocatively because, in the mind of a sick person, they will think the victim wanted that to happen to them. I was surprised. I haven't talked to my dad in a while, but I recall my last conversation with him as if it were just yesterday when he told me that he was proud of me. I responded, "Dad, I understand, and I forgive you. You can never go back and change the past. Yesterday is gone. Now what are you going to do with the rest of your life?"

I thought to myself, *Wow, when did your emotional switch just shut down? How could you not have love, a natural affection?* Today I understand that you can't give what you don't have. That's why developing a relationship with God is so important because the Word of God teaches us to love. I don't know about you, but I don't know where I would be if it weren't for the love of God. I needed him when I felt forsaken by my mother, abused by my father, confused by the world.

I share my story with you, sir, so that you don't have to repeat the words of my father. So that you don't have to live a reckless life. Daughters need their dads. I can't go back into my childhood or fix the damage that was done. Neither can you. But I tell you my story so that you can learn from the mistakes that others before you have made. Daughters need your love and support, so please don't violate them, for they look to you as their hero and their protector.

As a father, you are needed to provide your love in healthy ways. I will share a little bit more in depth how important it is later in the book. I wish I could explain to you the emotion I felt that day when my dad affirmed me and said, "Talicia, I am so proud of you. Because of the crowd that you ran with, I thought that you were finished." My dad went on to explain that his father was never really involved in his life. But what would have happened if he had sought out how to be a great parent, a good dad? What if he had tried to follow after the things of God? Surely, we can do it in our old age, but then it's too late because the damage has already been done. I told my dad, and I will tell you. Making a mistake is not the end of the world, but how you handle it from here has the capacity to change your life and those who are in it. So I say to you, move forward into your future.

The fact remains that even as I raised my own children, the way people treated me impacted my life as a parent. I was feeling so forsaken. The definition of molestation is not just sexual. I was so torn and broken until I began to break my own son down, not even fully aware of what I was doing to his spirit. I didn't molest him sexually, but I was so emotionally distraught that I molested him emotionally and spiritually. I really thought that molestation was only sexual. But according to Webster's dictionary, to *molest* can be sexual, or it can mean to harass.[3] Webster's define molest as: assault or abuse a person especially a woman or child sexually. The second definition is to pester or harass someone typically in an aggressive or persistent manner, to hassle, pester, bother, annoy, beset, persecute, torment. So parents, when you speak harshly to your children because you're stressed out by life, that's molestation as well.

Child to Parent Poem

Children and young people, love your parents;
one day you will wish you could.
I know they have made mistakes, done silly,
stupid stuff that they would change if they could.
Should you grow older, you too will see
that you didn't do all you should.
But at that point where you were in life,
you too will see that you've done the best you could!

Satan's Goal Is to Rob You

"For we are his workmanship, created in Christ Jesus unto good works, which God hath ordained that we should walk in them" (Ephesians

---

[3] *Merriam-Webster,* "molest (*n.*)," Accessed February 27, 2018, https://www.merriam-webster.com/dictionary/molest.

2:10).

Most people want to save face and are unwilling to acknowledge the mistakes that they have made. Some only acknowledge what others have done to them. But in order for healing and transformation to take place in my and my son's lives, I had to humble myself and admit my wrongdoing and repent to my son and to God. The Bible says in Matthew 5:23-24, "Therefore if thou bring they gift to the altar, and there rememberest that thy brother hath ought against thee; Leave there thy gift before the altar, and go thy way; first be reconciled to thy brother, and then come and offer thy gift."

We'll dive deeper into those verses a little later on. But the point I want to make here is that, for a long time, we have been called many names, names that have damaged our character, self-esteem, and self-worth. Many people walk around with a complex, not knowing or understanding how great they really are. Some know that they have potential but are so damaged by the negative things that people have said about them in ignorance, and those works have become a stronghold in their lives. John 8:36 says, "If the Son therefore shall make you free, ye shall be free indeed." People who have said negative things to you or about you might not even be aware that they were cursing you. From this day forward, my prayer for you is that you will walk in the commandment and in the obedience of God until all those negative curses and cycles will be broken off your life because of the anointing and because of your obedience to God so that the real you can come forth. In fact right now, in the name of Jesus, I call forth the real you. I decree and declare that every negative word curse that was ever spoken over your life be broken now in the name of Jesus. Where a curse was spoken, I decree blessings and favor to take its place. I declare that these things can no longer hold you and your family hostage. I decree that God is about to do a new thing in your life and all old cycles and dysfunction has been broken off your life. I declare that relationships that were stranded as a result of the enemy's attacks shall be restored and that the bonds of constriction will be permanently broken in the name of Jesus Christ. I decree a supernatural manifestation of the glory of God and for his glory to shine in you and in your future generations. I declare that interest be paid unto you and your children, according to Proverbs 6:30-31, "Men do not despise a thief, if he steal to satisfy his soul when he is hungry; But if he be found, he shall restore sevenfold; he shall give all the substance of his house." Job 22:28 tells us, "Thou shalt also decree a thing, and it shall be established unto thee; and the light shall shine upon thy ways."

Deal with It Now or Deal with It Later

While attempting to resolve my pain, I tried talking to my mom, but she was not equipped to handle my suffering. Talking to her quickly turned into an argument. I lashed out at her because I only felt worse. She couldn't provide the nurturing that I needed. Looking back, this could have easily been resolved as soon as she acknowledged what happened. What we are unwilling to confront will only build into a more negative force. But if we deal with things quickly, then the enemy cannot gain a foothold in our lives or in the lives of our children. My mom's bad choices became a problem for me, and as a result, these same issues became a problem for my son. If not dealt with properly, these issues have the potential to negatively affect his children too. Do you see that these issues can negatively impact generations? So here I am, raising a little boy who would one day become a man. I know some people would say that having a child at seventeen was not a great idea. I know that too. At least now I do. As a teen, I was so focused on growing up. Somehow I felt that the quicker I got there, the better off I'd be. So all I focused on was family and how I'd raise my family totally differently. But at the same time, I was becoming an abuser myself.

It was no good to have all that anger built up inside of me. I was so angry that I was like a walking time bomb, waiting to explode. So I'd drink. And when I drank, I felt like dancing and singing, and I was the happiest person. You'd think I was someone else. But when somebody made me mad, even the smallest offense would set me off. If I saw someone looking at me wrong, somehow I thought, *I wish somebody would bother me. When they do, it is on.* At times, I was so drunk, that I'd start fighting. One day, I woke up in jail, singing the song by Deborah Cox, "How Did You Get Here?" This song was a hit at the time that made my point. She tried love before, and it didn't work out. The lyrics fit my situation in a strange way. Circumstances of cause and effect can create a domino effect until the problems seem overwhelming. One bad choice leads to another.

During those times in my life, although I knew kindness was in my heart, it was buried deep within. I wish I could have been kind all the time, but because of all those open wounds, I couldn't. I would say to people, "No, that's not who I am but who you made me to be." Deep down inside, I wanted to express love; I just didn't quite know how. I sat in the house for days at a time, just wondering how I got here. Not in the physical sense but spiritually and emotionally. I felt dead. It wasn't to the point of wanting to commit suicide, but I had the idea of just swerving my car into other cars. But a little voice inside of me said, *No, I want to live, and I certainly don't want to hurt any innocent people.* How many times do we hear of tragic events when gunmen go into places, including churches, and kill multiple individuals, some who they've never seen before? One man was hurt by a lady and posted live while she was shopping and allegedly killed a man he didn't even know because of something his girlfriend did. I honestly believe that these people were decent people. I just believe they hit a very low point in their lives that required love, and they didn't receive it. No one reached them in time. I believe these people were crying out for love and to be loved in returned. Others had wronged them over and over again until they were at a point where they just couldn't take it anymore. I had days like that, thinking, *Lord, help me.* I cried and drank myself to sleep on many nights, asking God, "Why me?"

Never Forsaken

Even after everything I went through with my daddy, I was reminded of what the Bible says in Psalm 27:10. "When my father and my mother forsake me, then the LORD will take me up." The *agape* love of God will vanquish these things as well. I thank God for looking out for me for many years. Things like this go on in the house, things that no one desires to talk about or bring up. Keeping those things bottled up causes more harm than good. I told my mom about one of her friends who was molesting another family member. I didn't say that it was me because somehow we never want to hurt our parents with the truth, so we hurt ourselves instead. When my mom didn't believe me, I got mad at her. I knew it was true because he was doing the same thing to me. That created a wedge between my mother and me that remains until this day. Don't get me wrong, I understand that it's all over, and the past is in the past. But because of these incidents, I left home at fourteen. I ran into a lot of bad people, and if it had not been for the Lord who was with me, I could have been dead, on drugs, pimped out, and much more. These incidents robbed me of my childhood and my innocence. Family can be so ignorant and say the wrong things. Instead of making it better, they make it worse. They say things like, "Well if you were ten, you could talk.

You let that happen to you." They ignore the fact that you were young and impressionable and should not have been placed in that situation in the first place. So instead of being healed, you walk around with an open wound and appear to be overly sensitive. Have you ever had a small piece of glass or a splinter or even a hang nail, and someone barely rubs it? Oh, that hurts so badly. That's what those why those who have been violated feel because they have unresolved issues.

Chapter Two:
What Is Love?

"I will sing of the mercies of the Lord forever: with my mouth will I make known thy faithfulness to all generations"

(Psalms 89:1).

"Charity suffereth long, and is kind; charity envieth not; charity vaunteth not itself, is not puffed up, Doth not behave itself unseemly, seeketh not her own, is not easily provoked, thinketh no evil; Rejoiceth not in iniquity, but rejoiceth in the truth; Beareth all things, believeth all things, hopeth all things, endureth all things. Charity never faileth" (1 Corinthians 13:4-8a). We are all familiar with the word *love*. We all use it. Some of us might have studied about the various love languages, which help us in developing and maintaining love relationships. But much of the crisis we face in today's society is because, without God, we don't have the capacity to love as he intended.

A list of the various forms of love in the Greek follows:

•*Eros*:   Erotic love that you share between you and your spouse.

•*Philia*:   Affection

•*Storge*:   Family love

•*Ludus*:   Playful love

•*Pragma*:   Enduring love

•*Philistia*:   Self-love and

•*Agape*:   Unconditional love.[4]

Now we could dive much deeper into the Greek and the Hebrew and

---

[4] *Merriam-Webster*, "molest (*n*.)," Accessed February 27, 2018, https://www.merriam-webster.com/dictionary/molest.

define love, but the Lord instructed me to keep this book plain and simple. Our primary focus here will be on *agape*, which is the *love of God*. As a believer who walks in victory, power, and authority, you must be on guard so that the enemy does not rob you of love.

According to Webster's Dictionary, love is a strong affection for another arising out of kinship or personal ties. Maternal love for a child, attraction based on sexual desire: affection and tenderness felt by lovers. 3. Affection based on admiration, benevolence, or common interests, warm attachment, enthusiasm, or devotion, the object of attachment, devotion, or admiration.

The word *love* means different things to many different people, depending on where you grew up or your environment. What you place value on determines your perception of love. In some cultures, certain things related to love are more acceptable. For example, some cultures here in the United States might believe that anything goes and that everyone should be for him or herself and God for us all. You might even be familiar with the term that what's right for you might not be right for someone else. In fact, some think that they don't need love as they grow older because they can just love themselves. This self-aggrandizement, along with other false and preconceived notions of love, has caused the hearts of many to grow cold. God has made his intentions clear from the beginning when he commanded us to love him and to love our neighbors as ourselves. Many people think that they love others when they treat people with anything but love. So it's possible to speak words with our mouths yet have our hearts be far from it.

The *Agape* Love of God

This book is first written to the church folk, the religious institutions all across the world. It's not written as an insult, but it's written to remind us of the importance of fulfilling our mandate to love. Before we proceed, let's revisit the *agape* love of God.

The love that I'm speaking of is not an ordinary type of love, not the kind that starts out well and then leaves one's life shattered in a billion pieces. No, that's not the kind of love that I'm referring to. This love that I'm talking about is called *agape* love.

The Greek word for love is *agape*. According to Wikipedia, the Greek language distinguishes among four different meanings for the word love.

But as with other languages, it's been difficult to separate the meanings of these words when used outside of their respective contexts.[5]

For this book, our only focus will be on the *agape* love of God, which covers all the other definitions of love. *Agape* means love, charity; the love of God for man and of man for GOD. *Agape* is used in ancient text to denote feelings for one's children and the feeling for a spouse, and it was also used to refer to a love feast, like a communion meal. *Agape* is used by Christians to express the unconditional love of God for his children. This type of love was further explained by Thomas Aquinas as "to will the good of another"[6] as an unconditional love—a love that transcends and never ends; it keeps on giving and creating, adding and building up, yet never tears down.

Eros means *love, mostly of the sexual passion.* The modern Greek word *erotas* means *intimate love.* According to Wikipedia, Plato redefined his own definition; although *eros* is initially felt for a person, with contemplation it becomes an appreciation of beauty itself.[7] Plato does not talk of a physical attraction as a necessary part of love, hence the use of the word *platonic* to mean without physical attraction.

Agape love is a God kind of love, the love that God has intentionally placed inside of you. This love is not based on what it can get and does not love out of force but is freely given and received. The Bible says in Matthew 10:8, "freely you have received, freely give." How many believers walk around every day, thinking that it's impossible to have that kind of love? They feel as if people just won't allow you to love them as fully as you can and the way that the Lord has ordained. "A new commandment I give unto you, that ye love one another; as I have loved you, that ye also love one another" (John 13:34).

In fact, the scripture goes on to say that "He that loveth not knowth not God; for God is love (1 John 4:8). Why is it that we say *yes* to the Lord yet walk around in our hearts with unforgiveness, bitterness, jealousy, anger, hatred and strife? Then we have the nerve to justify our foolishness by claiming, "Well, I will just have to love some folks from a distance." The Bible tells us in 1 John 4:20, "If a man say, I love God,

---

[5] "Greek Words for Love," *Wikipedia*, accessed February 6, 2018, https://en.wikipedia.org/wiki/Greek_words_for_love.

[6] "Catechism of the Catholic Church," *Vatican*, accessed February 21, 2018,

[7] "Greek Words for Love," *Wikipedia*.

and hateth his brother, he is a liar: for he that loveth not his brother whom he hath seen, how can he love God whom he hath not seen?" In order to truly understand the love of God, as believers, we must go back to the beginning, a time before man was even created. A time before you were ever born. A time when time never existed.

Chapter Three:
What in the World Is Going On?

Any human with a heart that feels and eyes that see can easily take a look around our world and can clearly see that we are in trouble. A lot of activity is going on in the world, and the majority of it is bad, such as human trafficking, sex slaves, slavery, drugs, and alcoholism. There's so much confusion.

I believe that any time there's a lack of truth, there will always be confusion. This book is not designed to point out problems but to provide practical and biblical truths and insight as to why there's so much confusion and calamity happening in our world, communities, families, homes, and, yes, even within our own minds. The answer to *why* is most important in creating a solid foundation as to how to take a stand for yourself and your family during times of crisis and confusion. Once we understand why something is happening, we will begin to understand how to position ourselves spiritually, mentally, and emotionally.

The Bible was right and did not lie, for the hearts of man have grown cold and desperately wicked. Today the scripture is clear. Despite what we see, we can stand assured as long as we know and remember why these things are happening in our world. Then we'll know exactly what to do and how not to react but to counteract as we love in the peace that God has promised to allow his people to walk in despite all the calamities that might be transpiring in our world today. Anyone anywhere can take a look around and see all that's happening in the earth right now and see many situations that will cause one to shake their heads with amazement.

We're living in a day when it's difficult to trust. I can't trust them with my heart. What in the world is going on now? Every time I turn on the television, I hear more and more bad news—at home and at work. The crazy people at my job are always at each other's throats. We understand the fact that the Bible teaches that "man that is born of a woman is of few days and full of trouble" (Job 14:1). No matter your circle or your walk of life, no matter how many degrees you might have earned, you too understand that no one is exempt from trouble. It's so difficult to find any peace.

Chapter Four:
Is This Hell?

As I sit here, my eyes are filled with tears. My heart is regrettably full of deep sorrow. Not only due to the recent murders of African-American men across the globe but also the brutal murders of police officers. A recent murder also claimed the lives of at least fifty people in Orlando.[8] The list goes on and on with unnecessary pain due to the loss of many lives. As I try to digest all of this, my heart can't help but relate to the pain of losing loved ones who fell victim to the streets of Chicago and the familiarity of my own pain, the pain of my past. Oh, pain, how familiar and acquainted I have become with you!

The truth of the matter is that I started this book long before people began crying out in the streets about "Black Lives Matter." I agree, yes, they do. The truth is that all lives matter. As I sit here, I recognize the pain and can't help but reflect back on my own life. I know this pain all too well. It's no wonder the Holy Spirit keeps prompting me to finish this book. I wanted to wait, but the Holy Spirit says, "Now is the time of release. The world needs to know what I have to say about the situations that are occurring in the earth." The Lord wants all of mankind to grasp and understand the importance of my words. This word is not just for one specific ethnic group; this book is for all of mankind. No matter who you are, no matter where you live, you need to understand the importance of love—the God kind of love, the *agape* love of God. This love is unconditional. This love leads and guides you. This love shields and protects you; this love causes you to triumph even in the mist of fear. This love is a game changer; it moves you from victim to victor. This love never changes. This love will keep you. I know, for I am love. And love is cure. I cannot sit on this book any longer. The world is

---

[8] Ralph Ellis, et. al. "Orlando shooting: 49 killed, shooter pledged ISIS allegiance," *CNN*, June 13, 2016, https://www.cnn.com/2016/06/12/us/orlando-nightclub-shooting/index.html.

yearning for the principles that have already been written in the Word of God.

Please understand that I write this book from a perspective of my pain. Yes, I'm very acquainted with pain caused at the hands of others and even pain that I have caused myself due to wrong choices. At age seventeen, I lost my dear friend who was murdered in the streets of Chicago. By age twenty-six, I lost my fiancé, the father of my child who was two years old at the time. So the pain of death and losing a loved one due to violence is all too familiar to me. But that pain is only a corner of the pain that I can relate to. Today many people are wondering what in the world is going on, what's happening. The fact remains that there's an outright war between good and evil. This is a matter of the heart that should not be ignored. As we know, wars are fought for power, territory, and gain. This war that I'm speaking of is a war for the hearts of mankind.

Shawn's Death

At the time of my boyfriend's death, I had experienced the loss of close friends that were brutally murdered in the streets of Chicago. Back then, things were so bad that we had a saying: "It's a dog-eat-dog world out here, and only the strong will survive."

Violence was so prevalent in our community until it became a part of our norm. But at the tender age of seventeen, various outbreaks of shootings were taking place in my community just like in a combat zone; it was an all-out war. I learned the difference between fireworks on the Fourth of July and real gun fire. Out of all the warring that I saw in my community, two deaths hit me personally and were really close to home. The first was the murder of my boyfriend when I was a high school student. He was gunned down at a community park, and I was at school when I first heard about what happened. I rushed to the hospital immediately where I saw his body just lying there, lifeless. I had heard of many senseless killings prior to this, but this was the first time I had ever seen the body of a person I truly cared about. The second death hit me the hardest. My son's dad, Shawn, was murdered when I was about twenty-eight. His death changed my life forever.

He had called me two weeks prior to being murdered and told me that he saw death. I will never forget that day. During the phone call, he said, "Talicia, I really need to talk to you." I encouraged him to continue. "No,

Talicia, this here is really heavy and way out there. I think we need to talk face to face." I agreed and asked what it was about. He began to open up to me about his concern, and he told me that he was seeing death.

I was shocked and speechless, and my jaw dropped to the floor. He said, "Talicia, I hope I'm not losing my mind because I see death everywhere I go. I don't know what's going on with me. For example, you know that I don't do drugs, but I drink. Well one night on my way home, I hadn't had anything to drink at all. I was riding in the car when suddenly a guy just walked out of nowhere in front of my car. In order to avoid hitting him, I slammed on the brakes. I then got out of the car, looked all around, and looked under the vehicle only to find that no one was there."

Now as a young lady who had grown up in the church, the first thing that came to mind was what I said next. "Shawn, you have the power to rebuke death. Life and death is in the power of the tongue." Even so, I was at a loss for words. As I gathered my thoughts, I had to ask him, "Well, what does death look like?"

He said, "Talicia, it's hard to describe. You know that I'm about 6'2" and 180 pounds, but it's a shadow that's bigger than me, and it's been following me everywhere I go." As he was telling me all of this, I began to be overcome with fear and felt a strong negative presence, especially since I was at home alone, and it was beginning to get dark outside.

As Shawn continued to share his concerns, I was quickly dressing. I felt the urgency to go to my mom's because now I was afraid. Then I repeated to Shawn that we have the power to rebuke death. He responded, "Here you go again with that crazy stuff."

I told him, "No, really, it's true. At least that's what we were taught in church."

As soon as I arrived at my mom's house, I began to tell her what Shawn had shared with me about seeing death. I was waiting for her to tell me what to do. With a shocked expression on her face, she said, "We will be praying for him."

Two weeks later, I stopped by my mom's house where I was greeted by my brother Elijah. He stated, "Tee-tee, Shawn is dead." I laughed, hoping that he was joking again and thinking that perhaps he'd overheard me telling my mom about it.

I thought, *Surely this can't be true.* I tried to muster up a smile only to see that maybe my brother was serious about this tragic news. "No," I said. "I don't believe you. Stop playing like that. That's nothing for you to play about." My brother tried reaching for me with his arms outstretched.

He attempted to look me in my eyes and said, "I'm serious. Shawn is gone."

"No!" I yelled at him. I then questioned, "Where is momma? I don't believe you! Where is she?" He told me that she was at the neighbor's house, so I ran over there as it was less than fifty feet away. As I drew closer, my knees began to give out. I was trembling and weak but made it there. As I stepped into the house, somehow I was able to blurt out, "Momma, is it true? Is my brother is playing one of his jokes again?"

Momma just shook her head up and down without saying a word. I knew what she meant. "Yes, it's true. He's gone, Talicia."

I cried out again with a deep, deep "No!" from the pit of my belly and took off running from the neighbor's house. I just didn't want to accept it or believe that he was gone. I headed to Shawn's mom's house.

As I sat in my car, the conversation that he had with me that day about seeing death resurfaced to the forefront of my mind. I thought, *Wow, he told me. Maybe that was his way of warning me.* I went back over our conversation, thinking about all that he said. He even apologized for some things that he had done wrong. At one point after that, he came to my house and asked me to make him some bacon and eggs. Who would have thought that I could be so slow and unable to recognize the truth about the end of his life when it was staring me right in the face? As I digested all of that, I then began to examine my personal life and my own relationship with God.

I was born and raised in the church. But I will openly admit that I had doubts that God was really real. I felt that because I had never seen him, I inwardly questioned his reality. I wouldn't say that I didn't believe in God, but I didn't believe in religion. In my mind, religion was probably a system of rules to guard and keep the masses under control so that they obeyed the law. In other words, I thought it was possible that the government up made all this stuff about God. But now because Shawn told me that he saw death before he died, I knew then that there had to be some hard truth to the spiritual realm. In other words, he saw death and was dead two weeks later. I really needed to get my life in order because apparently God is real.

At the time, my life was a mess. I was drinking every day, all day if I could. I was wallowing in my misery. By misery, I mean that although I lived a street life as a drug dealer, I still had a taste of what it was like to work in corporate America. But now that I had a felony, I couldn't work the best jobs anymore. I felt bad because I had gotten involved with all those foolish things when I was just seventeen. But now that I was older, I knew better and knew the right thing to do. But I was now prohibited from being the best that I could be when it came to a job. All of this was on top of all those traumatic experiences that I'd gone through in my childhood years. At this point in my life, God began to deal with me, and I began to get my life in order. I began to come to the realization that it was time to give God a real *yes*, a *yes* that doesn't doubt, waver, or fear. This *yes* was from a place of truth. Although that was a very bad experience, my take away was that my faith and belief in God were verified and solidified.

Have you ever felt like there has to be more to my life than this? I was trying my best, and I was still not happy. I wanted to love the people in my life, but they just couldn't be trusted.

Another example of these struggles is the presidential election of 2016. Was that the weirdest election you've ever seen? After the 2016 election, my heart went out to Hillary Clinton who seemed so saddened by the loss. She looked exhausted. She worked really hard; she fought, and as badly as she wanted it, she seemed really hurt by the fact that she didn't win. This last campaign was very different. In fact, my first boss, Willie Wilson, also ran as a Democrat in this election.[9] That's how close to home this election was for me. Dr. Wilson's son, his own flesh and blood, came forward in the light of the media to say that his dad didn't take care of him. Instead of assisting his dad with the campaign, he wanted to shame him.

---

[9] Adam Gabbatt, "Willie Wilson: the Democratic party candidate you've never heard of," *The Guardian*, February 26, 2016, https://www.theguardian.com/us-news/2016/feb/26/willie-wilson-democratic-party-candidate-youve-never-heard-of.

Another shamed son, Danney Williams, appeared on "The Alex Jones Show," claiming that he is the son of President Bill Clinton.[10] He further alleged that he's been banished from having a relationship with his supposed dad, Bill Clinton. He believes that Hillary Clinton was keeping him from this relationship with his dad. This man says that he's contemplated suicide because people refuse to acknowledge that Bill Clinton is his dad. He finally asked for a DNA sample so that he can find out if his claims are true.

Danney Williams claims that he was forced to live in foster home after foster home while his dad was the president of the United States. This young man states that he's had a rough life. People teased him for saying that he was Bill Clinton's son, challenging the truth of his claims. I can't imagine what he experienced. Although Danney doesn't have a close relationship with the Clintons, he does report that Bill Clinton gave him some Christmas presents and money in his earlier years. But the gifts and money suddenly stopped. If Danney's allegations are true, his heart must be in a great amount of pain. Can you imagine going to bed hungry at night when your biological parent is the President of the United States? Can you fathom the hurt, pain, and agony this young man must feel, being born into that situation? This young man claims that he's has gone to bed hungry many nights, just trying to provide for his brothers and sisters. He says that he is really hurt by the Clintons' refusal to accept him as his biological son.

But according to Snopes, a DNA test has proven that Danny is not the son of Bill Clinton.[11] Even so, the questions surrounding his birth and upbringing have cast doubt on what the truth really is. Now my goal here is not to shame anyone. In most cases, the trouble in life started brewing long before you were born. Sure, we understand that sometimes people act irresponsibly, which brings pain upon innocent people. Sometimes things happen in life that are far beyond our immediate control. This is an example of how painful life can be for anyone, anywhere, at any time. Pain does not discriminate based on race or social class. Children are innocent, and it's a shame that they are caught up in the reckless results

[10] Staff Reporter, "Is this man Bill Clinton's love child? Prostitute's son says ex-President is his father and claims Hillary 'banished' him," *Daily Mail*, October 3, 2016, http://www.dailymail.co.uk/news/article-3819671/Man-claiming-Bill-Clinton-s-illegitimate-son-prostitute-continues-campaign-former-president-recognize-him.html.
[11] Staff Reporter, "Paternity Jest," *Snopes*, October 3, 2016. https://www.snopes.com/bill-clinton-illegitimate-son/.

of adult choices. I too am no exception; that's the reason I believe God has instructed me to write this book.

As I said before, I asked God, "Is this hell?" I felt like Job with one problem on top of the other; even my problems had problems. My life had gotten so bad that I thought this must be hell. What kind of world was I living in, and what kind of God would allow such pain? I told God, "I was an innocent child, and you allowed these things to happen to me. If this is not hell, then why haven't you answered me yet? Why do you allow the wicked to reign?"

Over the years, I looked at the actions of others and saw the condition of their heart. I saw hearts that were deceptive, envious, very hateful, liars, and yes even some backbiters, with every evil at work. Hearts that refused to allow the light of God's love to shine through because the love of God had been snuffed out of them through various trials and traumas. The enemy had stolen their love, and darkness had overtaken them. Some were in the church. They were white-washed tombs full of dead men's bones, men and woman with a "form of godliness, but denying the power thereof" (2 Timothy 3:5). These men and women were carnal, walking in the flesh. They had no real relationship with God. I'm not judging them; however, Matthew 7 teaches that we shall know them by the fruit they bear. These were not bearing the fruit of the Spirit; it was of a spirit but not the Holy Spirit. "But the fruit of the Spirit is love, joy, peace, longsuffering, gentleness, goodness, faith, meekness, temperance: against such there is no law" (Galatians 5:22-23). These church folk were not displaying the fruit of the Spirit. All I saw was envy, strife, argument, disagreements, slander, hatred, and everything our Heavenly Father forbids.

I also noticed that the people of God suffered hardships at the hands of the church. I too suffered. I went to the church and bought into the vision of the pastor. If the pastor had a vision to do what God had instructed him to do concerning the ministry, I prayed and attempted to work in assisting bringing that assignment to pass. But I almost always ran into opposition from those who tried to stop the ministry. They didn't want to do the work nor did they want anyone else to. I firmly believe these are instruments of Satan, used in churches all across the globe to prohibit the move of God. A short time later, the Holy Spirit began to teach me that not all who say, "Lord, Lord" are his. In other words, not everyone in the church is the church. Some folks are there on a specific assignment from the devil himself to stomp out the move of God. Others are there with a heretic spirit on a straight assignment to wear out the ministry gifts of that house until they become weary in well doing. In most cases, these individuals aren't even aware that they are being used of the enemy. At one time, so much calamity had broken out in the church, but the pastor told me that I shouldn't take it personally. At the time, I didn't fully understand what he'd meant. John 10:10 tells us that the enemy comes to kill, steal, and to destroy; the enemy comes after people because of what's in them. An evil spirit—not a person—is coming after you; therefore, you must attack the spirit, not the person, through prayer. The Bible says in 1 Corinthians 10:4-5 that "the weapons of our warfare are not carnal but mighty through God to the pulling down of strongholds."

God has selected some to be an example in the Body of Christ to exemplify the real love of God. God told me that he desires for you to be an example. He wants you to be the one that exercises his love. Walk in love; live in love. We have to be one with God in order to fulfill such an assignment. That's why Jesus said in John 10:30, "I and my Father are one." That's why, as the people of God, we must walk in the Spirit of God. Romans 8:14 tells us that those that are led by the Spirit of God are the sons of God. When we walk in the Spirit, we won't fulfill the lust of the flesh. (See Galatians 5:16.) We won't become easily angered or offended and will never become bitter. Instead, we only become better.

The world doesn't want to be a part of the church because we are too busy sacrificing one another instead of killing the flesh. We want what we want, and that's just the way it is. We don't care who suffers or how many lives are negatively affected as a result just as long as we get what we want. As the people of God, we must clearly understand the importance of this love walk. You can't tell me that people don't act like this in the church because I know they do. They act from spirits of witchcraft, jealousy, and strife. We have heard in Song of Solomon 8:6 that "jealousy is as cruel as the grave." These are spirits of control. As the people of God, we have to learn to acknowledge and address this love issue so that we are a prepared people.

The Bible says in Mark 16:15 to "go ye into all the world and preach the gospel to every creature." But it's hard to go because the saints will try to kill you if you do. Let me explain. They become jealous of the anointing that God has placed on your life and will murder your name, character, and reputation. Everyone wants their name in lights, and everyone desires a major platform. Everyone wants to be acknowledged by man. But when was the last time that we performed an examination on ourselves, according to the word of God? When was the last time we measured ourselves against the Word of God concerning our love walk? Do you mean to tell me that you'd rather look good in the sight of man than to have God pleased with you? I'm talking about the real you. You are who you are when nobody is watching. Or do you choose to be one of the ones who says, "Lord, Lord" but are none of his? My point here is, if you are in church and you have an issue with love, go to God and ask him to heal your heart, which is your soul. This is the seat of your emotions. Ask him to restore you. You can pray the following prayer. "Lord, build me up. Teach me how to love, remove anything that may be preventing me from your true *agape* kind of love. Lord, bless me to know who I am. Deliver me and restore my love, according to your original plan and purpose."

Chapter Five:
Love Them Anyway

The Lord, along with the presence of the Holy Spirit, had to usher me through some incredibly challenging times in my life. I went from being molested by my own father and step dad to being doubted for telling the truth by my mom. That felt horrible. I was hated by the majority of my siblings, so I knew what Joseph's life was like. I was slandered by loved ones whose duty it was to protect me, sold out by family, lied about by church folk. People were mad because I was ordained to preach the gospel. This wasn't the devil; this was his kids, those who posed as church saints. So here I am, and God's dealing with me regarding his people. In this season, God said, "Yes, I know what they said, and, Talicia Parker, I see what they have done. Now I want you to love them anyway!" I must admit that this was the end of my season of unforgiveness. You know the steps. At first, we're confused. Later we're mad, and then we accept the fact that they wronged us. Yet we still can't quite understand why. Then we move to accepting the wrong and we wait for an apology. They spent days, months, and years pretending that they haven't the slightest clue what we were talking about. Others spent time trying to justify their actions. So here I am, at the end of my healing process. I finally said, "Really, Lord. I love them."

He said, "Prove it in prayer. Pray for them." I was able to do that, and I prayed for all those who'd violated me. The Lord said, "You're ready. You still have your love intact." The Holy Spirit began to explain to me as he walked me through the course of my life. He showed me how, through all the pain, the enemy's goal was to steal the love from my heart. His goal was to lead men and women astray because of lack of love. The Holy Spirit informed me that there's a war going on for the hearts of man. And that's what this battle, all that warfare, was all about. He said, "Talicia, it was never about you personally. It was about your love."

Just in case you aren't aware of it, the role of the Holy Spirit is to lead and guide you into all truth. In fact, John 14:26 says, "But the Comforter, which is the Holy Ghost, whom the Father will send in my name, he shall teach you all things, and bring all things to your remembrance, whatsoever I have said unto you." The holy spirit is a teacher, a leader, and a guide. He began to point out patterns to me and events that occurred in my own personal life. If a person wasn't strong enough, the trauma would make them go crazy.

John 13:34-35 tells us, "A new commandment I give unto you, That ye love one another, as I have loved you, that ye also love one another. By this shall all men know that ye are my disciples, if ye have love one to another."

This is the same question I will put to you. What will you do with the rest of your life? We can't move forward when we continue looking back. No matter what you have been through, no matter what you might have done, you need to decide what you are going to do today. I urge you to shake it off. Forgive anyone who has wronged you. God will do great things in your life. But like me, get rid of the unforgiveness so that you can live a life of freedom and success.

Never be afraid to confront situations or people that have wronged you. Don't get me wrong. Sometimes people do things and are unaware that they have caused you pain. Others might try to deny the fact that they hurt you at all. If this happens, do what Dr. Wesley, my former boss, suggested I do. Imagine yourself telling this person, "I forgive you." Not everyone is willing to acknowledge the fact that they caused you pain, and that is okay too; it's not your problem that they want to live in denial. That's their problem, not yours. You must refuse to take personal responsibility for their inability to acknowledge their mistake. Never become upset if this person does not want to deal with it. Be sure that you don't carry the burden of "I can't believe they are acting like I don't know what I'm talking about." Don't carry the burden of them trying to flip responsibility on you. Don't carry the burden of them trying to tell you that you're crazy. Don't carry the burden of them accusing you of still talking about that old stuff and telling you that now is the time to throw all that behind you rather than admit it or acknowledge it. You move forward. Push past this pain. You have acknowledged it and have forgiven them. Now come to grips with yourself.

Empty Wells

One day, I had a dream. In this dream, my mom was sitting in front of two pots with plants. Mine had soil in it, and her pot was empty. I told my mom the dream, but at the time, I didn't understand it. While writing this book, God began to reveal the meaning of the dream to me and the reasons why so many people love inadequately. All the years I spent with my mom, I was so frustrated with her. She was a very sweet mom. Despite how wonderful she was to me, I didn't receive certain things from her that she just didn't have to give. I was attempting to draw from her, expecting nourishment. But God had to teach me that she could not fully nurture me because she herself was empty. My mom is a wonderful mom; however, she did not have what I needed. Not that she was a bad mom, but because people become empty after they have suffered and poured out. They have to be poured into. Can you draw water from an empty well? Can you give a million dollars if you don't have it?

It is impossible to love another unless you first love yourself. You can't express what you've never seen, received, felt, imagined, or understood. In other words, you can't give what you don't have nor can you draw from an empty well. That's why it's important to surround ourselves with positive people who mean to do good to us so that we can be refreshed. Proverbs 11:25b reminds us, "He that watereth shall be watered also himself." The Lord told me to tell you not to be upset with others or bitter because people just didn't have the capacity to love you properly. My coach, John Maxwell, often says, "Be a river not a reservoir," which means to be full so that you overflow.[12] We might be expecting to receive love from people that they just didn't have to give. I think that love is like a gas tank, and we must learn to keep it full. By surrounding ourselves with those that are of the household of faith, they can keep us charged. Don't surround yourself with empty people because they can drain you.

---

[12] LLC Meadow's Edge Group (Compiler), *Life Wisdom: Quotes from John Maxwell: Insights on Leadership*. (Nashville: B&H Publishing Group, 2014). p. 100.

Chapter Six:
Was that Pain
the Lord's Will for My Life?

After half of a lifetime of pain and disappointment after disappointment in my life as well as others, I thought about God's will. Sometimes we even hear people say, "Well, I was abused and molested or raped. Why did God allow this to happen to me?" What happened was man's doing, not God's. God is not the author of confusion. In fact, according to 1 Timothy 2:4, God desires that all people be saved; it's his will for all mankind. This is why God established the Ten Commandment to the people of God through Moses.

So what am I saying here? There are two wills of God—his sovereign will and his will of command. God's sovereign will is irrevocable, which means it can never be changed or altered, and it must come to pass. For example, Jesus, was the sacrificial lamb, had to be crucified. In Luke 22:42, in the Garden of Gethsemane, we find Jesus praying, "Father, if thou be willing, remove this cup from me: nevertheless not my will, but thine, be done."

We find the two different wills, Jesus's will and God's will. The sovereign will can't ever change, which leads us to the second will called the will of command. You remember the Ten Commandments, don't you? Of course you do. You also know that the Ten Commandments are broken every day all day. God has given us the ability and the authority to exercise free will. This is where the majority of all problems kick in. This is the root cause of all evil. This helps answer your questions of why the Lord allowed these bad things to happen to me, such as why I was molested. This helps answer why people are starving in this world and how people can be so mean and evil. This answers why people are placed for adoption and why life is so messed up. This answers why people could act this way and where God was when these things were happening.

When Pharaoh had to let the children of Israel go, that too was the sovereign will of God. The sovereign will of God can never be changed or altered. On the other hand, man's free will causes you to be wounded, hurt, and bruised. Man is wounded when man refuses to obey the will of command, such as the Ten Commandments. Had man acknowledged God's commandments, you and I would never have suffered harm. The will of the commands governs mankind on earth, but again each person has free will. The Bible says in Deuteronomy 30:19, "I call heaven and earth to record this day against you, that I have set before you life and death, blessing and cursing: therefore choose life, that both thou and thy seed may live."

We must first understand that we face a spiritual battle as earth's citizens. The Bible says in Ephesians 6:12 that we "wrestle not against flesh and blood, but against principalities, against powers, against the rulers of the darkness of this world, against spiritual wickedness in high places."

For many years, I battled with some, if not all, of those same questions. As I said, as a very young toddler, I was molested by my own dad, the man who God designed to protect me. Instead, he turned around and violated me. I have often heard that most children can't remember that far back; however, after I started to research and study Christian counseling and psychology, I learned that some children who experience trauma will remember these events because they are very traumatic. On the other hand, some people might unconsciously block out that traumatic event and choose to forget what happened. Most of those individuals who choose to forget those traumatic experiences become stuck. If left undealt with, these events and the related emotions will start to fester and begin to grow, basically creating a psychological and spiritual death from the inside out. This is the reason that we see so many individuals in the world with displaced anger, hate, bitterness, strife, and the inability to grow and become all that they can potentially become.

The truth of the matter is, if we ever want to be liberated and free from all limitations, we must face our hurts, fears, and monsters head on. You can't conquer what you can't confront. Believe it or not, some people, men especially, choose not to even talk about these bad experiences. Somehow a man feels ashamed or embarrassed to admit that someone violated him as a child. I have learned that talking is therapeutic. It grants a feeling of liberty and freedom, leaving us free from bondages that are associated with the pain of molestation, shame, guilt, or hurt. Talking helps us take our personal power back. For many years, I couldn't really love because I felt as if something was always holding my love back. Today I can easily see how it was the pain, the residue of being molested and feeling afraid, hurt, alone, bitter, disappointed, frustrated, and disconnected. I now realize that it wasn't until I was able to accept what had happened to me, forgive those who had sold me out, and remove myself from carrying these psychological bags of junk that didn't belong to me.

When an individual is molested, they have the tendency to think that maybe it was their fault or that they are unworthy of God's love. They might think they didn't deserve to have a loving father or that they're cursed. They might wonder why God allowed this to happen to them. But today I stand here to say that's not so. Hurting people hurt other people. Lost people will cause you to be lost, just like unloving people can cause you to be unloving. But thank goodness, we serve a loving God who's able to meet us at our very point of need. I thank him for meeting me and for helping me to overcome all negative experiences.

Psychologists say that there is no proof that children can remember. All I know is that I do remember being molested by my dad as a child. Was this the will of God? No, this was the will of my dad, who had a choice. My point here is that God is not responsible for the bad things that happen here on earth. "And God blessed them, and God said unto them, Be fruitful, and multiply, and replenish the earth, and subdue it: and have dominion over the fish of the sea, and over the fowl of the air, and over every living thing that moveth upon the earth," according to Genesis 1:28. But first, we must master coming into full alignment with the sovereign will of God. This is the whole duty of man. We must have a relationship with God in order to realize that, "If my people, which are called by my name, shall humble themselves, and pray, and seek my face, and turn from their wicked ways; *then* will I hear from heaven, and will forgive their sin, and will heal their land" (2 Chronicles 7:14, emphasis added). That scripture alone indicates to us that we are living in a very sick society and world. Whenever a man turns to molest a child that God has given him to protect, that's sick. Anytime a mother or father abandons his or her family, that's sick. Anytime we can witness third-world countries starve to death or go hungry, that's sick. When we see brutal murders in the street, that's sick. When police officers who are hired to serve and protect turn and kill the citizens that hired them, that's a sick society. When we see corruption in government, that's sick. The thought of all this calamity even as you watch the daily news is designed to promote fear in the hearts of mankind. In fact, if you listen to the news enough or watch social media, you just might be afraid to even go outside. And when you do go out, you might wonder at all the mess that goes on.

Every time we turn around, we hear of a bombing somewhere, of fighting for land and territory that's been stolen in most cases. Thievery is going on right before our very eyes; injustices are taking place right before our eyes. And what you don't hear on the news, you hear at work. Even your boss might be acting a little crazy. Everyone at work is scared to death, afraid to be thrown under the bus just so they stay on. If you manage not to experience this sickness at work, then just wait until you get home. You might even experience it in your own house with unnecessary arguments between you and your spouse or your children. As I mentioned before, it's no wonder why the Bible says that we wrestle not against flesh and blood. Notice that the scripture says *wrestle*. Yes, wrestle, as in a fight. You have to fight to get in bed at night and fight to get out of bed and fight on your job and fight through traffic and fight for safety in the community. You have to fight for justice to be served and fight to get to church and fight to stay in church. When you finally get to church to fight the good fight of faith, the church sisters and brothers want to fight who God called you to be. They want to fight your gift, and some fight the pastor; some fight in the choir, and they fight over positions. If you're not careful, seeing all this calamity can make you become hard, bitter, angry, or even afraid. As Paul tells Timothy, that's why we must only fight the good fight of faith. It's no wonder that the Bible instructs us to not even look at their faces. (See Jeremiah 1:17.) We must not be afraid.

2 Timothy 1:7 tells us, "For God has not given us the spirit of fear, but of power, love, and a sound mind." If you listen to the news for long, you will realize that the only remedy is love. The weapons of our warfare are not carnal but mighty to the pulling down of strongholds (2 Corinthians 10:4-5). What is this fight all about? What is the calamity and the wars and the rumors of wars all about? Why is your own sister jealous of you? And why can't you get along with your own mother? Why did your daughter sleep with your husband? Why can't your husband remain faithful? What is that witchcraft stuff all about? Why are people trying to hurt one another? I'm going to repeat myself here. There's a lack of the

agape love of God.

With all of those negative experiences in my life, these questions ran through my mind. Were all of those bad experiences the will of God for my life? Why did God allow these bad things to happen to me? Does God hate me? If God is so good, why do I hurt so badly? If there is a God, then why did he let this happen to me? Sometimes these questions come up in our hearts and minds. I'm sure that, if you've ever been hurt or wronged, you have asked yourself these questions too. Lord, why me?

Chapter Seven:
Why Don't I Feel Loved?

Do I Really Need Love?

You'd be surprised at the number of people who think it's okay to live a life without love. These individuals never express love or affection. They have a callous heart that has become so hurt and hardened by life's disappointments. Some are even bitter. These individuals have built walls around their lives so that no one dares come close to them. These walls don't let people trust or allow heart-felt communication or emotional connection. Forget about being optimistic because of the fear of being hurt again. These people have determined in their hearts that love just doesn't exist, is not real, or is overrated. These people are not free to love as there's no emotional access to their hearts. We don't have access to liberty. We can't reproduce what we've never seen or heard. Because most of us have not properly received love, we can't properly give love.

Loving yourself is vitally important; however, before you can love yourself, you must know and accept who you are. Truth be told, most of us suffer from an identity crisis. We don't know who we are; we don't believe in our capabilities. We are not sure of our strengths and weaknesses. We're afraid to allow others the chance to see our flaws. That's the reason for the cover up. We cover ourselves in makeup, clothes, and jewelry because we have not accepted the fact that we are not perfect. We don't love ourselves. We hide behind our accomplishments and success. We hate others who we feel might be doing well or who might have better opportunities. All because we don't know who we are. I can easily tell if a person knows who they are based on the way they treat others.

Chapter Eight:
Love Is Cure

Where do evil, hate, lies, and deception come from? Surely, we must get to the root and to the heart of the problem. In my opinion, if you are a human being, then there is good and bad in all of us. There are two natures in mankind, a good and bad, an upper and a lower nature, a king and a fool inside of us. There is no such thing as being born bad or totally evil. Though sometimes men sink to the lower nature, there's no such thing as being totally rotten to the core. The good is there, buried beneath hurt, disappointment, fear, rejection, and every evil work. In fact, if you show me an individual whom society deems bad, I will clearly ask the person to take me to the spot where they lost their goodness. Was it just one incident that caused their goodness to be hidden or was it a series of negative events that occurred over time that has somehow forced goodness out of its rightful place due to an absence of love? See, love and goodness can be strained, crushed, or bleeding out gradually over a period of time. As a woman, daughter, and mom, I've experienced love just starting to ooze out of me, sometimes after a bad experience of hurt, pain, shame, betrayal, and disappointments, just to name a few.

Life has so many ups and downs until sometimes individuals become hurt, disappointed, rejected, or denied the proper cultivation to maintain a great flow of love. Many times we're unwilling to give love in places where it might not be reciprocated. Where there is no goodness, then there's an individual who lacked love at some point or another.

The Bible says that man ". . . cometh forth like a flower, and is cut down: he fleeth also as a shadow, and continueth not" (Job 14:2). This verse is something to think about; we can clearly see that. At various points in life, they experienced a life-changing traumatic experience.

Have you ever wondered how or why wars begin? How is it that people in families fight among one another year after year, generation after generation? How is it that a man decides to kill another man? How is it that mothers are against daughters and fathers against sons? How is it that a father or uncle whose responsibility is to provide, protect, and direct the lives of a child then turns around and molests his own sons, daughters, nieces, and nephews? How is it that a husband and wife turn into enemies? There's so much calamity in our world. It seems as if those who were supposed to love shifted us into phases of hate, and people become immersed into sinfulness of the heart. Instead, we should walk in the natural affection of loving those that God has placed in our lives to care for.

What's This Love Thing Anyway?

According to Webster's dictionary, love is an intense feeling of deep affection, fondness, tenderness, warmth, intimacy, attachment, endearment, to adore, idolize, worship.[13] Webster's definition is not far off from the biblical definition of love found in 1 Corinthians 13:4-8a. "Charity suffereth long, and is kind; charity envieth not; charity vaunteth not itself, is not puffed up, Doth not behave itself unseemly, seeketh not her own, is not easily provoked, thinketh no evil; Rejoiceth not in iniquity, but rejoiceth in the truth; Beareth all things, believeth all things, hopeth all things, endureth all things. Charity never faileth."

Most people have been denied love for a long time. They have decided to believe the false statement that love is only a four-letter word. It's no wonder that my grandmother use to quote a scripture from the Bible. She'd say, "And be not conformed to this world: but be ye transformed by the renewing of your mind" (Romans 12:2). As I grew older, I understood what grandma really meant.

Where there's an absence of God, you can also expect an absence of love. The Bible says that God is love and that whoever does not know love does not know God, because God is love, and we have known and believed the love that God hath to us. (See 1 John 4:8.) "And we have known and believed the love that God hath to us. God is love; and he that dwelleth in love dwelleth in God, and God in him" (1 John 4:16). For God so loved the world that he gave his only begotten son, that whosoever believeth in him should not perish but have everlasting life (John 3:16). To me, it's clear that, according to John 3:16, love is

---

[13] *Merriam-Webster*, "love (*n.*)," accessed February 25, 2018, https://www.merriam-webster.com/dictionary/love.

sacrifice. Not the kind of sacrifice where there's a shedding of blood, but a sacrifice that results in the act of giving up something that you want to keep for the sake of a better cause. This means that, in order to live life in its fullest form, one must be willing to sacrifice what he or she might selfishly desire so that others might reap the benefits. According to the scripture in 2 Corinthians 5:21, "For he hath made him to be sin for us, who knew no sin; that we might be made the righteousness of God in him." This means that Christ unselfishly bore our burdens so that we might inherit eternal life. No wonder the Bible also states that "greater love hath no man than this, that a man lay down his life for his friends" (John 15:13). People are perishing every day due to a lack of knowledge concerning love. This is primarily due to a lack of understanding that, when you have love, you have God, and when you have the love of God, you have everything because God is love. Love is the key that leads to a life of joy and happiness for all who exercise it. In John 13:34-35, Jesus leaves a new commandment to "love one another" as part of his final instructions to the disciples after the last supper ended and after Judas Iscariot departed. I believe that Jesus was showing the disciples that, as long as you follow the principle of love, you will fulfill the entire law of Moses. Why? Because love will not allow us to act selfishly.

What is love anyway? I must admit that when I read the scripture in 1 Corinthians 13, I said, "Well, that leaves me out." This scripture allowed me to examine myself. I saw that I lacked patience because patience means the capacity to accept or tolerate delay, trouble, or suffering without becoming angry or upset. My problem was when it took people too long to understand what I meant, I became upset. I thought people should know what I meant, but people might not be there yet. How many know that we can be right and wrong at the same time? I became upset when people took too long to catch on. Instead of becoming upset, I should have prayed that the Lord would open the eyes of the people so that they could comprehend. Today my prayer is that God's people will have eyes to see and ears to hear what the Spirit of the Lord is saying to the church. How many know that the church doesn't even have this love thing down pat yet? And we must have love—the *agape* kind of love down pat. Not love as the world loves based on human emotion and how others make you feel. But the kind of love that is always willing to give, willing to accept, willing to forgive, willing to forebear, willing to restore, willing to go the extra mile, willing to let the other person go first, willing to be kind, willing to sacrifice, and willing to love. The reason the world is held back is because most of the church folk are holding them back simply because we have a love issue.

Chapter Nine:
Judgement Begins
in the House of God

As the people of God, the chosen of God, you have been given a mandate to love. People all over the world are seeking the face of God, saying, "I'm just trying to fulfill my mandate, my God-given assignment, but some are attempting to fulfill it without fulfilling God's first mandate, which is the mandate to love. His mandate on our lives is to be the example of *agape* love. I firmly believe that's why ministry gifts are graced by God—to help ourselves and others endure hardships, persecution, lies, slander, abuse, and much more. God has graced every ministry gift to be overcomers. Just as Jesus Christ himself overcame the world, we too as the Body of Christ must overcome the world's challenges. We must be that example and make a firm decision not to live a life of defeat but a life of victory in Christ Jesus. In life, we will suffer many tribulations and many hardships, but God has equipped us to endure every test and trial. At various times in my life after suffering hardship after hardship after hardship, all I could see was pain. I suffered so long and hard that pain went as far back as I could remember. I suffered so much until I had to seriously enquire of God.

We were designed to love because God is love, and no matter what the world is doing, no matter what things might look like in life, never lose God's real agenda, which is to love. What is love anyway? Is it overrated? Why do people fight against love yet long to be loved?

In the scripture in John 13:34-35, Jesus said, "A new commandment I give unto you, That ye love one another; as I have loved you, that ye also love one another. By this shall all men know that ye are my disciples, if ye have love one to another." Most people will argue the fact that they have love. But let's look at what love is anyway. Here in the scripture, Jesus says love one another as I have loved you. Then the next question should be, "How has Jesus loved us?" He loved us so much that he gave his life for us, which means that love is sacrifice. What is sacrifice?

According to Webster's Dictionary, the definition for sacrifice is the act of giving up something that you want to keep especially in order to get or do something else or to help someone. : an act of killing a person or animal in a religious ceremony as an offering to please a god. : a person or animal that is killed in a sacrifice.[14]

That's what the kind of love that comes from God will cause us to do, to deny what we want just to look out for the best interests of others. We will put our families and our neighbors first. True love is placing the needs of others before our own.

In today's society, the hearts of people have been conditioned to do just the opposite. No wonder the Bible says in Matthew 24:12, "And because iniquity shall abound, the love of many shall wax cold." We can see that this has already begun.

We've somehow disregarded the fact that God's Word instructs us to love the Lord thy God with all our hearts and love our neighbors as we do yourself. But we fall short of the glory of God because we also miss the loving God. (See Mark 12:33 and Luke 10:27.) It's impossible to love others without first loving God. This love moves beyond the emotion and moral affection of love that's called *phileo*. Do you not know that, no matter what is going on in the world in our relationships, God intended for us to live in peace? Apart from God, we can do nothing.

We all have challenges and worries, such as delivering a healthy baby or being a good provider, especially as a man. We all have hopes, dreams, and ambitions too; we want to do well. We want to be successful. We would like to send our children to a great college or university. We want a great career and to buy a beautiful home with the white-picket fence. We too want to live the American dream.

I call them survival challenges. Those challenges can be that you want your children to do well, grow up safe and healthy, and live a better life than you did. You want your generation to supersede the last and to leave an inheritance to your children. Why isn't life happening that way?

Psychologists commonly state that hurting people hurt other people;

---

[14] *Merriam-Webster*, "sacrifice (*n.*)," accessed February 24, 2018, https://www.merriam-webster.com/dictionary/sacrifice.

wounded people wound other people, and broken people break other people. We are all a product of our environment. How we grow up and the condition in which we grow in shapes our perspective and how we view the world. Our perception is our own personal world view. It's no wonder we hear the common statement, "You won't understand my story until you've walked a mile in my shoes."

What is love anyway? Most people don't know what it is. Some people repeat the words, "I love you," just because you said them first. It's almost an automatic response. But far too many people have no idea what these words mean. Some will say that love is just a four-letter word. Others think it's for the ladies, so they might even use tactics that manipulate others. If they had a lot of problems, they think that love would solve them. No wonder the Bible tells us, "I live by the faith of the Son of God, who loved me and gave himself for me" (Galatians 2:20b).

Chapter Ten:
Understanding Your Identity

I woke up from a dream, screaming, "Who am I?" In this particular dream, I was in a park, flying a kite. All of a sudden, this unfamiliar man walked up to me and said, "You know, there's a lot that you can do with your hands."

I responded, "Of course. I can clap them, snap my fingers, pop my knuckles. wiggle my fingers, and wave them too." I looked away from him in total disregard, thinking, *Please, tell me something I don't know.* I ignored him and went back to flying my kite.

This strange fellow then tapped me on the shoulder again and said, "No, you can do a lot more with your hands." He then instructed me to drop slowly and lower my hands from top to bottom with my fingers spread apart. Out of curiosity, I did what he said. As I began to lower my hands, the lower I dropped them, the higher up in the air I went. Suddenly, I was looking at the tops of trees. Although this was only a dream, I can still feel the shock of levitating in mid-air because of the motions I made with my hands. Then this strange fellow instructed me to do a different motion that allowed my feet to safely return to the ground. Once on the ground again, I stared at my hands in shock. *I didn't know that I could do that with my hands.*

This stranger then instructed me to begin waving my hands in a certain motion. This caused the trees of the field to begin moving in the direction of my hands. I know it sounds weird. I was kind of shaken too. In this dream, I was so shocked to learn what I could do with my hands. I wondered who this stranger was that knew about my hands, things that I didn't even know about myself. Now I wanted answers. This man then tapped me again and said, "You don't know who you are, do you?"

I answered, "Yes I do. I'm Talicia Renee Parker, daughter of Elijah and Gaye."

He then tapped me a third time and yelled, "No, you are not! That's not who you are!" He took off running. I took off running after him. He was so fast. I reached after him and grabbed a hold of his vest. He then pulled his arms out one at a time and escaped and continued to run.

I could not catch him. I awoke screaming and chasing after him, "Who . . . am . . . I?" At the time, I had a very little indication that I'd been called to the ministry. In the days of the prophet Elisha, he had the prophet Elijah to train him, according to 1 Kings. During that time, I had little or no training. Since then, I have begun to learn who I am. I began to learn and understand destiny. I began to identify my gifts, and I began to understand who I was.

I have been called many names, some of which are improper to repeat. Some of you can relate to this. The fact remains that society has also tried to label you and I with many names. I can hear God's voice softly speak, "Never mind what the world called you or what they labeled you. You are who I say that you are!" You are who God says you are. You are not what you have been through. That's what God wants me to tell the world. You are not what you have been through. You are not pain, shame, or confusion. You are who he called you. "Before I formed thee in the belly I knew thee; and before thou camest forth out of the womb I sanctified thee, and I ordained thee a prophet unto the nations." According to Ephesians 3:17, I am rooted and grounded in love because Christ dwells in me (paraphrase). Some of us suffer from an identity crisis that can also prevent us from loving others. Not knowing who we are, what we're here for, or understanding our significance here on earth can become a love issue. What does that have to do with love? Until you understand who God created you to be, you will compare yourselves to others, which allows jealousy and covetousness to work its way into your heart. If you're not careful, you'll look at your life, circumstances, challenges, victories, and defeats and began to compare them to other people's lives. But God does not want us to do that. He wants us to be content in our own skin, knowing that we are fearfully and wonderfully made by God himself. You'll even look at their gifts, and instead of appreciating what the Lord is doing in the lives of his people, you'll start to envy that gift. Instead, you should allow yourself to be blessed by their gift. After all, the purpose of every ministry gift is a gift from God to you. Before long, that envy grows, and you began to reject the gifted person and the gift of God.

The Real You Is Hidden Deep Inside

The real you is hidden inside of you. Will the real you please stand up? Will the real you please come forth? The truth of the matter is that the real you is hiding from a world full of trouble. The real you would rather not deal with all the calamity, all that hurt, and confusion. It just wants to stay hidden. You can't even allow yourself to be nice to others because people often mistreat those that are nice. I even recall a trainer saying, "Well, I'm not nice; I'm kind." You might even be familiar with the saying that people take kindness as a weakness, so you don't want to be labeled as kind.

We live in a world where the identity of people is controlled by other people. Anytime you allow your real personality to be hidden from people, you are under their control. They—not you—control your emotions. The real you is hidden beneath all the cares and concerns of this world. It is hidden beneath all that you have endured, all that you have not resolved, and all that you have been unable to let go of. The real you is hiding just like Adam hid in the garden the day that the Lord looked for him after Adam had sinned.

Adam was ashamed and hid himself because he was afraid. He was embarrassed because he was naked, disobeyed God, and was also afraid. That's how the troubles of this life can leave us, hiding and not knowing what to do next. Instead of running to God, we run as far away from his presence as we can. We leave the real us, our spirit man, buried beneath all that we either refuse to deal with or perhaps just don't know how to deal with. As I said, for many years, I had displaced anger. I knew I was angry; I knew why, but I just didn't know how to quite deal with it.

"Then the LORD said it is not good for man to be alone. And the LORD God said, It is not good that the man should be alone; I will make him an help meet for him" (Genesis 2:18). We see here that the Lord created male and female, and that it is was not good for man to be alone, so he made man a helper. And Adam called her Eve. In the beginning, the Lord blessed them and placed seeds of multiplication in and around them. They were to "be fruitful, and multiply, and replenish the earth, and subdue it" (Genesis 1:28). God had given them dominion power. But something went wrong in the Garden. In the Garden, we see the enemy at work and interfering with the love that God has for man. The goal of the enemy was to get man to sin and to go against the plans that

God had for man. The enemy's job was to get them to fall into disobedience. Isaiah 1:19 says, "If ye be willing and obedient, ye shall eat the good of the land." So in the beginning, the enemy tricked both Adam and Eve to do something that God had commanded them not to do. We are still dealing with these things to this day. We can see that the enemy is interfering with love. He interfered so much that they were kicked out of the Garden of Eden. If you allow the enemy to trick you, he will cause you to lose ground. He will attempt to get you thrown out your own Garden, the promises of God.

As believers, we understand that there is a remedy to restoring our love and bringing back God's intended plan for our lives and for our families. 1 John 3:8b says, "For this purpose the Son of God was manifested, that he might destroy the works of the devil." As believers, don't allow the enemy to come in between marital relationships. It all starts with the man. Men, you are the head of the house; you are the king and the captain. If the family is going to be exceptionally blessed, then, you, sir, must remember God's original plan for your life and get back to the basics. That's why there's so much temptation coming up against the man. There is pressure of all sorts coming against the hearts and minds of man, attempting to get you to forfeit the promises of God for you and for your children. There's temptation everywhere, just like in the Garden. As a man, the head of the family, don't look at the temptation but focus on what is at stake, focus on what's on the line. Remember that the enemy's goal is to take territory from you and your family. He desires to get you all kicked out of the promise. The wife serves as your helper in the fulfillment of the mandate that God has given you. Proverbs 13:22 tells us that a man will not only leave an inheritance to his children but to his children's children. And God is counting on you to multiply that which he has entrusted to you.

Therefore husbands love your wives as Christ loves the church (Ephesians 5:25). In fact, if you and your children are going to possess the land and hold fast to the promise and multiply, then it starts with you. Don't allow the enemy to gain a foothold into your family. You, sir, are the head and not the tail, above only and never beneath, the lender and not the borrower. (See Deuteronomy 28:1-14.) God is expecting you to obey his voice so that you and your family may eat the good of the land. (See Isaiah 1:19.) You, sir, are not your own. Everything you do determines the future and destiny of future generations. So hold fast unto the love of God. Teach it to your children. God chose Abraham because he knew that he would teach his children to honor the word of God.

The enemy is a liar and a thief who works contrary to the plans and purposes of God for your life. His goal is to trick you into believing the lies that are spoken, thought, and even acted out against you by you and others. His goal is to get you in agreement with his schemes, getting you to buy into the lie. In this life, most have suffered so much. Some things were out of our control. We unintentionally created some troubles because of our lack of knowledge. Some of you have been called so many names so that you don't have the slightest idea of who you are anymore. Some of you have even agreed with the adversary and have spoken all sorts of negative things out of your mouth. The enemy's job is to rob you of your true identity and get you to agree with what the naysayers have said.

You need to pursue the identity that God has created for you to walk in. The enemy's goal is to get you to deny who you are in God by getting you to agree with him and his agents. Jeremiah 1:5 says, "Before I formed thee in the belly I knew thee; and before thou camest forth out of the womb I sanctified thee, and I ordained thee a prophet unto the nations." That means before you ever were held in your parents' arms, you had an identity and an assignment to fulfill in this earth realm. And since all these troubling and traumatic experiences have occurred in your life, it has somehow tainted your true identity. The goal of the enemy is to wipe out not only your generation but your children and your children's children and their children on down. His goal is to negatively affect you and your blood line, but the devil is a liar. Don't you dare agree with that liar. God told Abraham in Genesis 12:3, "And I will bless them that bless thee, and curse him that curseth thee: and in thee shall all families of the earth be blessed." Don't go against what God has said or say things like, "Nobody will ever love me. Maybe I am just like who they say that I am."

"I don't even know who I am anymore. I feel like I lost myself along the way." Does that sound familiar? Our words are power, and they are life. Proverbs says the tongue has the power of life and death, and those who love it will eat its fruit. (See Proverbs 18:21.) How many of us have used our tongues loosely or have had those that are around us speak many negative things? The truth is that our words have no geographical limitation and will seek to accomplish whatsoever we say even when done out of ignorance or unbelief. How many times have we said things out of anger? Examples might be:

- Ya'll gone now
- Get up outta my face
- Ya'll putting too much pressure on me
- I'm so sick of ya'll or
- I don't know what to do.

Do any of these sound familiar? The spirit of doublemindedness seems to hit you. You're moody all the time—one minute, you're happy and upbeat, then the next minute, you're snapping at everyone.

On days like this, I drank and drank until I fell asleep. Some days, I just sat and felt sorry for myself. I rewound my years of hurt and allowed them to replay in my mind day by horrible day. I thought about all of the people who hurt me. I wondered for hours how they could do this to me. I questioned what kind of world we were living in. I just felt so numb at times. I sat and daydreamed about all those traumatic events of the past for hours. I guess that I was somehow looking for resolve, and I couldn't seem to find any peace. Some days, I just yelled harsh, cruel words to my oldest son because I was so hurt and broken and lost, living with displaced anger, just like a loose cannon. My words crushed my son's spirit even though I love him dearly. I didn't know what I was doing, but I said things to him like, "You're stupid," and similar dumb and mean statements. I spoke from displaced anger, all because I was so entangled in the past. I didn't understand what I was doing then, and I have asked God to restore my son.

Chapter Eleven:
Church Hurt and Forgiveness

Your actions can leave this gifted person wounded, offended, and hurt. This is what people mean when they talk about church hurt. The purpose of every ministry gift is to sharpen and prepare God's people. Instead, God's people are being wounded by the shepherd. Jeremiah 23:1 warns them, "Woe be unto the pastors that destroy and scatter the sheep of my pasture! saith the LORD." The purpose of scattering the sheep is to smite the shepherd. How do we get rid of this self-inflicted wounded spirit? First, we must begin to understand why the Bible says that we are all members of the Body of Christ. We all are one with Christ as the head. We must pray that God raises up some leaders, some apostles, some prophets, and teachers that will do their job of helping the Body of Christ identify their gifts, talents, and abilities. An apostle has been gifted to point out and activate your gifts. They can point you to purpose. They can clearly see who you are and what you're gifted to do with 20/20 vison.

What does this have to do with love? As long as you don't understand who you are, you can't walk in your purpose. You won't be effective in ministry; you'll always have a problem with other people, which will affect the way you treat them. If you don't know who you are, you will wound others. You can't love anyone else until you love you and until you understand your personal uniqueness. For example, is a tire a steering wheel? Is your car radio a phone? Can you use your steering wheel as a spare tire? No. You can try; however, I don't think you'll get very far because that's not the design of these things. As the people of God, we need to be more accepting of the gifts of God and get in the Word of God, which will enable us to know and understand our purpose and who we are. As we recognize our own gifts and potential, then we will identify the gift of God in other people. Then love is activated so that we can accomplish the work that needs to be done in the kingdom.

Many of you are just like me. Ever since you can remember, the enemy has been after your love. You have faced trouble from your youth. You've experienced various challenges, setbacks, mishaps, wounds, and insults at the hands of others. You've dealt with the thoughtlessness of others, been rejected, been lied to, mistreated, molested, violated, and misunderstood. I have dealt with all of these things too. But what if I told you that the whole purpose behind all of these attacks was due to the fact that the enemy was after my love? He's after your love too. As I mentioned already, the Bible warns us that the hearts of man will grow cold. This means that people won't care about anyone else besides themselves. I too couldn't understand it for years, but, thank God, he began to teach me that the enemy was after my love. God is love, so the enemy is after the God in me. He knows that, if he removes the God in us out of us, then we're left defenseless against him.

What if I told you that there's purpose for your pain? And what if I told you that the reason you've had all of these negative things happen to you was to be an example of what love really looks like, what love really feels like, and what the power of love can really produce? These things were totally out of your control but will be used by God. Many of you might have felt the same way and wondered why God picked you to be an example of his love. You wonder why you always have to take the high road. When I heard those words, the voice of the Lord said, "Because I know what I put in you! I know what you have the capacity to tolerate. I know the grace and favor that I placed upon your life. And with me, you are more than a conqueror." I pray that you will become the instrument in the earth that God uses as a tool to teach others because God is love. Love is the antidote to many challenges, plagues, war crimes, murders, suicides, and homicides. Love is cure!

This particular scripture comes to mind. As Jesus hung on the cross, he prayed "Father, forgive them for they know not what they do" (Luke 23:34). I can relate to this prayer, and I'd like to share this with you. In most cases, people have no idea that they are trespassing against you. I really believe that people have no idea of the amount of pain they might cause another to endure. It's as if they are not themselves. As an adult, I worked for a psychologist named Dr. Wesley. One day, I ran into his office with tears falling form my eyes. I asked him, "Am I crazy?" I began to explain to him all that I had endured. I shared the personal things that happened to me as a toddler.

He replied, "No, Talicia, you are not crazy. But if you want to move forward, then you will have to forgive your dad and anyone else who has wronged you." I told him that my dad did not even know that I remembered this as I was just three years old when this happened. He said, "Well, you have to go to him and tell him that you forgive him. One way to forgive him is to imagine yourself there with him, acknowledging his wrong. Then tell him, 'I forgive you.' It's just that simple."

Can you imagine how many people walk through this world each and every day, bitter, and unhappy because of the unforgiveness that torments their soul and spirit? Some are angry and have no idea why; others know why and haven't any idea what to do about it. The solution is that you have to forgive each and every one who has ever hurt you. There is freedom in forgiveness. Forgiveness is for you and for the person. This is a way of regaining your personal power.

My Ministry Story

Lots of issues with church hurt are going around. I too have experienced this, shortly after I finally built up enough nerve to accept my call into the ministry. I ran from the call of ministry on my life for years. In fact, the first time I accepted my call, I was sitting in a jail cell in the Illinois Department of Corrections. I ran from God for so long.

I ran because I didn't want the weight or responsibility of ministry.

I ran from the call because I felt unqualified.

I ran because I felt that there was no way that God could ever use a broken-down woman like me.

I ran because I'd been in and out of relationships; I'd been molested.

I'd never been given the chance to give my virginity away as it was taken from me, and I didn't even know when. I knew that the Lord loved me, but because of all the hurt I had endured, I felt as though I needed a drink of alcohol daily just to cope with all these disappointments. So there I am, sitting in a jail cell. The Lord reminded me of the call one day when I went to court. I was there with other ladies, and we had formed a prayer circle. I told all the ladies there, "Let's pray for your release." Apparently the prayer worked for them because everyone went home but me.

In that bittersweet moment, God began to deal with my stony heart and reminded me, "Talicia, you have to do ministry."

I agreed. "Lord, I've heard all of this before from prophets of old. I just don't think I'm your girl. Look, after all that has happened to me, you don't want me. I'm messed up." I even told the Lord, "*No, no, no!* Maybe one day soon, but not now."

The Lord then asked me, "Talicia, why do you think you were the one to pray for these women?"

I said, "Because that's what I know to do."

He said, "You see, I allowed all of them to go home just to show you that your prayers were effective."

I asked, "Well, why didn't I go home?"

He answered, "Because I need to speak with you. You have to answer your call."

I said, "Lord, I can't see it." The Lord allowed me to continue to sit in the county jail for the next forty-five days. I wasn't released until the word of God had really begun to prick at my heart.

There, the Lord revealed to me in a sure voice, "Whom I call, I qualify. Talicia, I am your qualifier, and before I formed thee in thy mother's womb, I knew thee and ordained thee as a prophet to the nations." (See Jeremiah 1:5.) I agreed that I would do ministry. Then I suddenly went home. And, boy, was I happy.

But I still didn't answer the call. I started making excuses like, "Okay, Lord, you know that I'm a heavy drinker. I want to represent you well. I will answer as soon as I stop drinking." But this took me years. At this time in 1998, I was still out of church. I didn't accept my call as a minister of the gospel until 2005.

I was in this church on fire for the Lord, when, suddenly, all sorts of confusion began to break out—not with the lay people but with leadership. I watched leadership break into arguments. I was also working in the church at the time. I watched powwows among the leadership. The church had the possibility to grow, but the evil forces that attended there didn't want growth and opposed anyone who dared to help. You have seen them as well: the church people that are old and set in their ways who don't want to do anything. They don't want you to do anything either. Sad yet true. Since there was no room for growth, I eventually outgrew the church and found another place of worship. This time, I decided to attend a relative's church in support of her and her husband. After all, we were family. When I had my businesses, this sister reached out to me.

I was attending there, and everything seemed to be going well. At the time, the pastor was the only active person in ministry in the church. One day, the pastor and his wife requested a meeting with me. At the meeting, the pastor and his wife offered me a position in the church as the assistant pastor. Since the Lord had already placed this on my heart, I was already prepared to give an answer. The only part that troubled me about the meeting was that the first lady initially had a problem with it. She said that she wanted to be the assistant pastor. I was hurt because she was not just a first lady to me, but she was also my younger sister. But I quickly got over it.

Before long, other relatives were upset over the fact that I had been given a position of ministry. I witnessed so much demonic activity beginning to take place. The enemy obviously did not want me in that position. One day after a church meeting, the pastor (my brother-in-law) said, "Talicia, I want you to go and buy a cassock." I asked what that was. He said, "It's a priestly garment." I asked what I needed it for. He told me, "I'm going to have to go ahead and obey God. People will just have to be mad at me." I knew that he was referring to my family. I felt a little sad and agreed to go and buy it.

Later that day, I phoned him and asked what color and what kind of cassock I should buy. He gave me the details and asked me to pick up two more, one for him and the other for my sister. I agreed. After I got there, I informed him that one of them was extremely big and would have to be taken in, but it was the last one they had in the sizes that he had requested. Once I completed my purchase and left, I thought, *Yes, I will finally be installed.*

The following day (Sunday), I was scheduled to preach before being installed. This was customary, and I did better than I expected. But I saw a lot of demonic activity in that service, and the air was thick with it. As I was preaching, I heard whispers. But no one in the services was whispering. It was a backbiting spirit, which I later learned about during my tenure in the school of ministry. During the service, my sister was leading praise and worship. The church deacon gave word that the pastor wanted me to come into the office to get dressed for the installation service. So I went to dress, and as the deacon was assisting me, I noticed my sister come into the office to get dressed also. I heard the pastor tell my sister that the apostle who was going to do the installment said that the Lord said that there were only two people that he should install. Not three. I heard them going back and forth. I didn't want to eavesdrop, but I overheard the pastor say to my sister there weren't enough cassocks. Apparently the apostle who was doing the installation needed one for himself. I had mine on, and I was so little that neither one of them could fit into mine.

I couldn't hear all that was happening, but my sister began to try on different choir robes. She has a strange look on her face, and the pastor looks like he's afraid. From there, I put on the robe as quickly as I could so that they could privately come up with a solution. Apparently someone wasn't getting installed that day. It was time for the installation to begin during the middle of the service. The pastor stood in front and called me to his side, and my sister came to his side as well. I didn't know what the solution would be. All I knew is that the two of them received their installment as I just awkwardly stood there. Don't get me wrong. I understood that the pastor and his wife were in between a rock and a hard place.

Why did they take me through such a horrible experience? On top of that, I was out $193.00 that I paid for all three of the cassocks. And I wasn't even installed. I was left feeling like a fool at the altar. Looking back, it's funny. I stayed on board at my family's church for about eight more months. Things didn't change, and I saw that they refused to obey God. I began to think back and examine my life. Looking back now from a place of victory, this awful experience is funny because I learned that we have to obey God no matter what. I got the pastor to sign off on my school of ministry paperwork. I then attended Living Word Christian Center School of Ministry as the Lord had already been instructing and confirming me to do. See it wasn't the fault of my sister or the pastor that I had that bad experience because I allowed my emotions to rule my judgment. God had already instructed me to attend Living Word for their School of Ministry, but I decided instead to wait and see if they would be obedient.

Once I left, I felt rejected by them yet not by the Lord. I've learned that when people reject you, it's only because they're afraid of you and don't have the capacity for you. But as a child of God, the Word clearly tells us that we'll be persecuted for righteousness's sake. In 2015, I was obedient and went where the Lord instructed me to go. I hadn't seen or talked to my sister for years. In 2017, I moved to a new town not too far from where they live. The day of the closing, I decided to drop by my sister's house, she and the kids were so happy to see me. And I was happy to see them also.

My point here is that things will come up in church, things that will hurt us. But, thank God, they won't kill us. We have to endure hardships like a good solider. And at the end of every test, there's a greater reward for them that remain standing in the faith unmovable, always abounding in the Word of the Lord. By the end of the test, you will notice that you're wiser, stronger, and better. And yes, you must forgive. Jesus was a great example of this forgiveness. As he hung on the cross, he prayed, "Father, forgive them for they know not what they do." That's a clear and attainable example of how Christ overcame the world, and so can we. I did it, and so will you. Don't allow anyone or anything to make you bitter. Hold your peace, and let the Lord fight every one of your battles. If you do, his Word promises that you will come out with victory. That's why we must forgive.

There's an all-out war going on for your love!

Satan's plan since even before time was to build himself a kingdom. He wanted to destroy God's goals for mankind. "And there was war in heaven: Michael and his angels fought against the dragon; and the dragon fought and his angels, And prevailed not; neither was their place found any more in heaven. And the great dragon was cast out, that old serpent, called the Devil, and Satan, which deceiveth the whole world: he was cast out into the earth, and his angels were cast out with him. And I heard a loud voice saying in heaven, Now is come salvation, and strength, and the kingdom of our God, and the power of his Christ: for the accuser of our brethren is cast down, which accused them before our God day and night. And they overcame him by the blood of the Lamb, and by the word of their testimony; and they loved not their lives unto the death" (Revelation 12:7-11).

In scripture, Satan was thrown from heaven and took one-third of the angels with him. He told God that he would build a kingdom greater than God's and that God's people would worship him. So this battle has always been about the love of God because God himself is love. The point I'm trying to make here is that Satan has always been after the heart of man and the love of God. That's why there's so much havoc in your personal lives and so much demonic activity at work. Satan is launching these attacks with the hope that you will eventually give up on the love of God and begin to take vengeance into you own hands by attacking those around you in word and deed. Don't fall for the deception. If we do that, he laughs at us and says, "Look, she doesn't have the love of God in her." The Bible tells us in Romans 12:19 that God will take vengeance and that he will repay evil to those who hurt us. 1 Peter 3:9 also teaches us to not look to repay evil for an evil committed against us but return good to those who might have violated, hurt, or wronged us in any way.

"To whom ye forgive anything, I forgive also: for if I forgave anything, to whom I forgave it, for your sakes forgave I it in the person of Christ; Lest Satan should get an advantage of us: for we are not ignorant of his devices" (2 Corinthians 2:10-11).

One of the goals of the enemy is designed to get you to retaliate. If we do, we have given in and chosen Satan's plan instead of keeping God as our first choice. In other words, you just gave up on believing God and instead became an advocate for the enemy. When you retaliate against people for hurting you, you surrender your love to the enemy who now has dominion over your actions. You become a slave to sin.

Take a look at Adam and Eve in the Garden of Eden. Satan's goal was to rob mankind. He tested the love and loyalty that was shared between Adam and the God of his creation through tricks. People, it's time to stop allowing the enemy to trick you out of your love. This *agape* love is not solely meant to be shared with God alone, but this love is a kingdom experience that refuses to allow the enemy to sell you out against God. No matter the circumstances in your life, you are determined to remain in the *agape* kind of love. No matter what the trick the enemy might attempt to use by getting people to hurt, bruise, or wound you, refuse to relinquish your love. When I have God and his *agape* love in me, I have everything I need in order to be a whole person with a kingdom experience and with his kingdom working with me. I then become a kingdom citizen of heaven with full benefits as a son of God. This kingdom experience comes with dominion power—the same dominion power that is the right to rule, the same power that Adam lost in the garden. This dominion power is activated because of my love for God.

What I'm saying here is whatever you do, no matter what happens in life, no matter who attempts to hurt you, hold fast to the *agape* love of God. This love makes you unstoppable. This love assists you in getting more done in less time. This love causes you to operate supernaturally in this earth. Don't lose your love because love is cure! Without the *agape* love of God, you will operate under the curse of Adam and Eve. The curse caused Adam to have to earn and work hard to till the ground by the sweat of his brow in order to eat. Before the curse, before Adam chose Satan's side over the love of God, he didn't have to till the ground. His provisions were automatically given to him just as surely as the grass grows in your yard. That's how God created seed to multiply inside of seed.

From the Hood to Opening my Own Businesses

By the time I reached the age of twenty-nine, I managed to open up a couple of businesses on the West Side of Chicago: Tee-Tee's Hot Dogs and Daedell's Barber Studio. I was doing well, considering how my life had started out in the beginning. But I still had unresolved issues. We all know that if you leave a food item in the fridge and never touch it, it will soon start to rot and smell bad. That's how unresolved issues of life are. If left undealt with, things will start to rot. If we don't deal with issues, they will show up in your marriage, house, children, in your actions, and even in your reactions. These issues can appear when you're alone even during times when it looks like things are coming up roses for you.

How did I go from dealing drugs to opening a business? I am not trying to pass the buck; however, when you grow up in a dysfunctional household with abuse, you want to leave as soon as possible. I left home because of the sexual molestation I suffered from my stepdad. This left me with the option of moving in with my grandma, which was where my dad was also living. In my mind I thought, *I'm older now. I don't think my dad will try to violate me at this age.* But in any case, I no longer wanted live with my mom and her boyfriend and planned to leave. At the age of twelve, I told my pastor, Bishop Burgess, that if my mom decided to stay with my stepdad, I would leave as soon as I was done with elementary school. Looking back now, that was a tremendous burden to put on the shoulders of a child. But I just didn't want to be under the same roof with an abuser and a manipulator. There was no peace; they argued too much and couldn't work together on simple projects as basic as going to the grocery store without fighting. Even at a young age, I knew my mom was a good woman, but this guy had her all confused. He didn't help her in any way that I could see. In my opinion, she'd be better off without him. She had all of these children (eleven), and because he didn't help her, that left me to take up the slack as the eldest. I simply grew tired of their negativity. I wanted out.

After the eighth child was born, I left. Parents must realize that what negatively affects you will affect you children, and whatever helps you will help them. In this case, I felt that I was better off out of that house. But leaving home at such a young age was like running from the skillet into the fire. A short while after, I moved in with my granny, my dad's mom, Willie Mae, who owned a two-flat building on the West Side of Chicago that she shared with my aunt. My aunt had eight children as well; however, they were around my age and a little older, so I would have very little or no responsibility in caring for them.

But as I said earlier, my dad lived on the second floor with my granny, and I stayed downstairs with my aunt and her children. My little cousins became very afraid at bedtime and wanted to sleep near the wall. When I offered to trade places with them, I found out why. My dad was molesting them and coming into the basement in the middle of the night.

After dad realized that he couldn't get in thru the basement door, he then attempted to climb through the window. I was at a loss for words. I had to place a 4' by 4' piece of wood in the window and hope that he couldn't open it without waking us up. Of course he tried; however, I had a broomstick and was basically fighting him off all night. I sat there and wept. I could only imagine what my aunt's children had to endure just trying to get a decent night's sleep. I pitied them. I often wondered if this was why their mom suffered from mental illness.

The next day, I got up and called my uncles and cousins over and began to explain all that had occurred that night. My uncles dealt with him, yet my granny somehow stayed in denial perhaps because my dad was her youngest child.

One day, a cousin from out of town visited granny's house. I was so worried about her, wondering where she would sleep. That night, I encouraged her to either sleep with my granny or sleep down stairs with us. I guess I thought I could protect her. At the time, I was a young teen and didn't really know how to tell a distant relative girl that if she stayed right here, she wouldn't sleep well. So I tried to warn her in a roundabout way. At the same time, this was my family, and I had been trained not to talk about what went on. Grown-ups always told me, "What happens in your house stays in your house."

So my cousin Brenda was probably uncomfortable with sleeping downstairs with a woman who talks to herself with a house full of kids. She decided to sleep on the living room couch, which was right outside of my dad's bedroom door. The next morning, I flew upstairs to check on Brenda. Based on the look of shock on her face, I knew that she didn't sleep at all that night. I asked her if she was okay, but she didn't respond right away and just stared. Later she stuttered, "Whhhhaaatttt be going on around her atttt niiigghtt???" She didn't have the words to express herself. I asked her if he touched her and told her that was why I suggested that she sleep with Granny or with us.

My granny overheard the conversation and said, "I don't believe that nobody did anything to you!"

I was furious. I said, "Granny, it's true. You have to believe people when they tell you the truth. Stop defending him if he's wrong." Eventually, I felt uncomfortable living there and began to just stay out all night. I started drinking more because deep down inside I was secretly worried about my brothers, my sisters, and my cousins. I don't think I had the room to worry about myself.

So I started to date a big-time drug dealer who treated me well, bought me car, and paid for a nice apartment. I was sixteen and working at a McDonald's owned by Dr. Willie Wilson. The job was set up through my high-school work program. (I was later kicked out for poor attendance.) I left my granny's house and never went back home. In the beginning, I was an excellent A-B honor student and president of the student council. I conducted various speeches for my school and attended the school's spelling bee. I took school seriously. My teachers told me that education was the key to success. Today I understand what they meant. But as an adolescent, I just couldn't see it.

The first successful African-American man I met was Dr. Willie Wilson who owned several McDonald's franchises. Up until that point, I had never before met a successful black man. In my eyes, they were all losers. There were no strong male role models to look up to. I was so excited, and Dr. Wilson really inspired me. Although I worked for him off and on for years, I only read about him. I didn't have the chance to professionally interact with him until I was twenty-four. And, boy, was his training tough; this is what I yearned for all of my life. I was from the hood yet full of potential. But by the time I finally had the right information, it was already too late. I had already been arrested for selling drugs. While working for Dr. Wilson as a crew manager and an administrative assistant, I was going back and forth to court. One day, I forgot to attend court.

I read about Dr. Wilson in the *Wall Street Journal*. He also sang gospel music and had his own orchestra. Although the pay at McDonald's was low, Dr. Wilson inspired me. He went from picking cotton to becoming one of the first African-American men to own a McDonald's franchise. But because of the low pay, I quit working there. I idolized big-time drug dealers. They owned companies, houses, and land and appeared to be successful. So I was dating this drug dealer and decided that I wanted in. I started by helping pick up money and making some drops. I wanted to branch out and have my own territories. Well now, I was known as what we call *ghetto fabulous*: we have the money and fame, and everyone knows your name. But I was arrested so many times for everything from mob action to driving without a license to having the wrong license plate on a car and, of course, for drugs. At seventeen, I was caught with drugs.

Out of nowhere, the Lord began to deal with my heart. I began to see that the life of the streets was not all that grand. The guy that I was with was now on drugs. I tried drugs as well but looked in the mirror and didn't like who I saw or who I was becoming. I prayed, "Lord, please don't allow me to get hooked on drugs." Later, I called my mother to come and pick me up after fighting with my drug-addicted boyfriend. I had had enough of the street life and wanted to go home. My stepdad and my mom had split up, so it was safe to go home. My mom and sister came to get me. I went back to McDonald's, and Dr. Wilson and Joyce began to train me. I had tried drugs, but, thank God, I never got hooked. But I believe if I had not prayed that prayer and if I had continued to indulge, I would have been strung out. I had to cut many people out of my life in order to make that transition and break from that lifestyle.

I was now working at McDonald's. Whenever people from the community saw me, they were shocked and asked if it was me. I proudly smiled and answered, "Yes, it's me, and I'm happy and free. I thank God because I'm still alive, and I made it out of that lifestyle." My goal was to own my own McDonald's. Instead at age nineteen, I began working for a Fortune 500 insurance company in corporate America. I was making around $26,000 annually, which was great for a teen at the time. I met lots of wonderful and professional people that were kind and patient with me.

From the guttermost to the utter most, love lifted me. No matter who you are, no matter where you may find yourself at this particular time in your life, you can rest assured that love has the power to lift you out of any challenges or circumstances. The love that I mostly refer to here is *agape* love, unconditional love. *Agape* love is the goal that God expects his children to establish and execute in the earth. Not the *phileo*, which is an emotional kind of love based on the actions of others. For example, this kind of love likes the way you make me feel. We get along well because we agree. *Phileo* is not the kind of love that God intended for us. Instead, he has given us the power to exemplify *agape* love in the earth. *Phileo* equates to the world's system of what love is. No wonder the Bible tells us in Romans 12:1-2 to not be conformed to this world but be ye transformed by the renewing of your mind. The scriptures also instruct us not to render evil for evil, because that's the world's way. (See 1 Peter 3:9.) As children of the Most High God, we must render good to others at all times. Based on the level of poverty I was raised in and the opportunities that I've experienced coming out of those poor circumstances, I can clearly see the correlation between the absence of love and poverty.

The Spirit of the Lord took my mind back to Matthew 18:21-22 that says to forgive seventy times seven per day. I must confess that it wasn't until the Lord revealed why we must forgive one person that many times that I was able to understand true forgiveness. Therefore, in order to truly exercise *agape* love, we have to forgive seventy times seven per day. The Lord revealed to me why he said this: this allows you to leave plenty of room for error. Forgiving others will prevent strife from entering. The enemy gains entry into our lives through offense and the spirit of strife. God knows that, if we allow or permit strife into our lives, then the enemy will begin to disrupt, distract, and tear down our lives. You can't focus on what's good because your mind is so upset with the way someone has mistreated you, so you continue to relive these bad moments in your head over and over again. In doing so, you put things that should be a priority and at the forefront of your assignment on the back burner. You leave these things. Then before long, you realize that a lot of time has passed. Strife and offense robs you of time. When strife enters your system, it has the potential to poison your mind, body, and spirit. Many people have diseases because of food, yes, but many diseases are due to strife and offense as a result of unforgiveness. Disease is exactly what it says—*dis ease*. So now not only will unforgiveness rob you of time and peace, it can even rob you of life and health.

You have to also learn to forgive those who are not sorry for their actions, those who might never apologize. Yes, even the ones who deny, deny, deny—those that are in denial about all the things they have done wrong to you. They deny the pain their actions caused, the price you paid, the sacrifices you made, and the inconvenience that you suffered. In fact, some will go as far as pretending that they don't know what you're talking about as if it never happened. That is a low blow, and then they will try to call you crazy, which is just like adding fuel to the fire. You're already heated up about the situation, but it has the tendency to become turned up even more when they call you crazy because they are in denial and are attempting to play mind games with you. Allow the Holy Spirit to free you today.

Chapter Twelve: Love Is Key

As parents, we must provide love and an accepting environment in our home for our children. If we don't provide a loving and safe environment for our children, then we unintentionally push them outside to fill that void from others in the streets. That's why young men join gangs and young women end up in abusive relationships or even become pimped out. I understand that, as parents, we're trying to do what's right, but if we become too preoccupied with foolishness or even with work, the enemy can steal the hearts of our children away. Therefore, we must be accountable to our families first. If we don't tend to them, the streets are more than happy to do so. The problem in the inner city is that we lack leadership. I'm talking about hands-on leadership that the community can connect with. We must have this connection—a sense of similarity in order to grasp the attention of inner-city youth and parents alike. We need the sort of leadership that has not forgotten what it means to be without, what it means to have hope, dreams, and information that will cause an individual to rise from their current mind set.

I developed a mentality of "trust no one, suspect everyone, and get them before they get you." Looking back, I see that I was looking for acceptance, looking for love in all the wrong places. Looking for the love I felt I never had. All I could think of was starting a family. Why was I suffering so much agony and pain? You might have asked this same question a time or two in your life. I can assure you that the answers are here to heighten your awareness, and they will awaken you. We will help you to discover the reasons why these things happened to you. We will uncover truths that will take you to a new level of understanding.

Really, so much negativity is going on in this world until it leaves you just waiting for the next big tragic event to occur. I can personally connect with the familiarity of my own pain, the pain of my youth. This word is not just for one specific ethnic group; this book is for all of mankind—no matter who you are, where you live, how many degrees you have acquired, your social class, or even your culture. It doesn't matter if you're nine or ninety-nine. God wants you to understand the importance of love. Sure, you might have come across quite a few books on love, but none like this, for it was written under the inspiration of the Holy Spirit himself.

The Enemy Is After My Love

Why is there so much calamity in the world? Every time we turn on the news, something catastrophic is taking place. There are wars and rumors of wars, wars in our country, wars in other countries, terrorist attacks, racism, families fighting, and people killing one another in words and in deed, for money and for position. The sad part of it all is that this same spirit has crept into the church. The very house of God which is meant to heal people now hurts them. Motives were somehow switched. Those who were intended to help others cause problems because of greed, hate, deception, and wickedness. At the same time, those who need God's help and favor are being hindered. Why? The enemy is after the love of God in your heart; he doesn't want you to understand or know your true identity. He knows if you ever find out who you really are, then you wouldn't feel jealous of others. You must know that the enemy's goal is to complicate your life, family, home, community, city state, nation, and the world.

That's why it's important for us to develop a personal relationship with God that's not based on man. Man will disappoint us. Psalm 118:8 instructs us not to put our trust in man. Hebrews 13:5 says that man will leave us, but God will never forsake us.

The enemy knows that as long as you don't have love, you will never reach your fullest potential with the Spirit of God enabling you to do the impossible. When you have the love of God, you have everything you need. The love of God will teach you how to love and appreciate others. Then they too will learn who they are.

Love sounds so cute. To some, it might be a joke or a fairytale that we choose to no longer believe in. We hear the word so often, and some take it for granted. Most don't know that it is an action word, which is a verb. You remember first learning of love, don't you? Think back to the day that you always dreamed of love and living happily ever after. What happened to happily-ever-after anyway? Don't worry, I'll tell you.

Happily-ever-after died when love left. Without love, there can be no happily-ever-after either.

Little Did You Know

At times, I cried and wondered why I cared about people: those that I know, love, and respect and some I don't even know. How is it that I continue to love those who have hurt me, criticized me, rejected me, talked about me, and those who have violated me and lied about me? I asked God if I was a fool on several occasions. How can I want the best for those who don't love me? As I mentioned before, the Holy Spirit took me to the scripture that says don't return evil for evil but return good for evil. He told me, "My daughter, I have selected you to write this book because of your heart." Then he took me to 1 Samuel 16:7 that says that man looks on the outward appearance but God looks at the heart.

Allow me to paint you a bigger picture. Many people focus on the outward appearance. I'm a beautiful young lady who understands that there's more to the outward appearance than anyone I know. I have been mistreated by other women in the church and the professional arena just for being beautiful. But the sad part was that they didn't know my story. These women had no idea of the hell I was experiencing because they only looked on the outside. On the outside, I was beautiful, but underneath, I was broken and shattered. So I say to women all over the world: we don't need to be jealous of people because of the way they look. You have no idea what's going on in the lives of beautiful women. These women didn't know that I grew up in the inner city of Chicago, the eldest of eleven kids, bullied in the projects, and sexually abused by my dad.

I was working several jobs, trying the best I could to make it as a single parent, trying the best I could to deal with my childhood giants. I dealt with inner turmoil. These women had no idea that although I was beautiful, I was shattered. I might have been beautiful, but I was broken, broken into pieces. These women had no idea that I was holding on by a single thread and was trying to pull my life back together again and allow God to repair my broken spirit. That's why it's so important for women to understand that they need to be comfortable in their own skin. There is no need to roll your eyes at a sister just because you think she's cute. Conquer that demon spirit and tell her, "Girl, you sure do look nice." James 4:7 says to resist the devil and he will flee.

See love and goodness can be strained, crushed, or bleeding out gradually over a period of time. Life has so many ups and downs until sometimes people become hurt, disappointed, rejected, or denied the proper cultivation necessary to maintain a great flow of love. Where there is no goodness, then there's an individual who at one point or another lacked love. And at some point in life, they experienced a life-changing, traumatic experience.

Job 1:6-12 says that Satan went into the presence of God, and God asked him where have you been? He then took that time to attack Job. 1 Peter 5:8 tells us that Satan is as "a roaring lion who walks to and fro, seeking whom he may devour." Now let's take a look at what the word *devour* means for a minute. According to Webster's dictionary, the transitive verb *devour* means to eat up greedily or ravenously, to use up or to destroy as if by eating, to prey upon. To afflict, consume, plague, defile, trouble, overcome, overwhelm. To destroy completely. To consume or destroy with devastating force, to swallow up, engulf.[15] This sounds familiar, right? Isn't that exactly what the enemy's attempted to do in our lives?

Now some of you are probably like me and asking what kind of God would allow the enemy to devour us. Why doesn't he just shut Satan down and be done with it? Why does it seem like this is some kind of game that I have no control over? God in his infinite wisdom knows all things, and therefore we don't understand everything today, but we will understand it all by and by as time goes on. Isaiah 55:8-9 says, "For my thoughts are not your thoughts, neither are your ways my ways, saith the Lord. For as the heavens are higher than the earth, so are my ways higher than your ways, and my thoughts than your thoughts." God knows the way we should take and after we've been tested, we shall come forth as gold. (See Job 23:10.) His *shalom* peace means that nothing is missing, and nothing is broken.

According to the Word of God in the book of Job, God begins to question Job and asks Job if he knows where he houses the rain or where the hail is kept. In most cases, God places us in situations to become good stewards. Look at the story of Joseph's life. (See Genesis 39-50.) He was hated and put in a pit by his brothers. Potiphar's wife lied about

---

[15] *Merriam-Webster,* "devour (*v.*)," accessed February 1, 2018, https://www.merriam-webster.com/dictionary/devour.

him. Finally, he was promoted as the second-in-command next to Pharaoh.

Daniel was placed in the lions' den because he refused to stop praying to his God. God then caused the jaw of the lion to be locked, and Daniel was still alive the next day when he too received promotion. (See Daniel 6 and following.) Shadrach, Meshach, and Abednego were placed in the fiery furnace because they too refused to bow down to any other God but the God of Abraham, Isaac, and Jacob. (See Daniel 3.) They also survived the fiery furnace and were not burned or consumed, yet they too received promotion.

You can see the pattern. You don't have to wonder about what life brings but know that God is a deliverer of his people and always causes us to be triumphant over all the schemes of the enemy. Life consists of cycles, circles, and levels. The Bible says that we will go from faith to faith and from glory to glory. In other words, we don't get to walk into higher levels of dominion and authority until we pass the test. For example, in school you can't move to high school until you have met all the prerequisites of eighth grade. You have to pass the test. When you pass, you will be promoted.

Growing up in the local assembly, the saints of old would sing, "I'm a Solider in the Army of the Lord." That song is true for many that have walked this earth. We can sense that there's constantly a war going on— if not here, then somewhere nearby. There's always a war brewing. If not on our own soil, then we hear of rumors of wars in other lands. If not at work, then at school; if not at school, then at home; if not at home, then at church. We face battles of the mind and battles within ourselves. Sometimes we face battles on every side. Then the people we come in contact with on a daily basis also are dealing with the same set of circumstances.

And God forbid that you start warring with someone who has wars going on in every frontier of their lives. This is why we must learn to yield our hearts and minds to the care of the Most High God. He is the only one who's able to keep us in perfect peace. We must also know that the battle is not ours to fight, but the battle belongs to the Lord. (See 1 Samuel 17:47.) "For this purpose the Son of God was manifested, that he might destroy the works of the devil" (1 John 3:8b).

If we ever want to be free and to live a victorious life, we not only need to know the problems that might plague our lives, but we must also begin to question why these things are happening in our lives. Why have they happened to others? What's going on, and what must I do to become victorious? What you went through did not kill you, therefore, you must learn to allow it to build you. Don't allow what you've gone through to hold you hostage or in bondage. Since it has not killed you, you must master it by learning to let go of every hindrance that tries to bind you up. "Thou therefore endure hardness as a good soldier of Jesus Christ" (2 Timothy 2:3).

Chapter Thirteen:
Living Dead

Do you have any idea of how many folks are living life yet dead? They walk around, moping and complaining all the time. Everything in life seems to be an issue for them, and all their problems are magnified. But whatever you look at the longest becomes strongest in your life. That's why before you go to bed at night and as soon as you open your eyes, you should focus on the Lord. "Keep thy heart with all diligence; for out of it are the issues of life" (Proverbs 4:23). I know you're probably thinking, "Well, what does my heart have to do with my mind?" You are more than just a body or a physical being; you're actually a tri-part being, created in the image of all mighty God: spirit, soul, and body. Our spirit is God-conscious; our body is sense-conscious (the five senses); our soul is self-conscious (mind, will, and emotions).

One day, I woke up and made my fresh cup of coffee as I always do. Then I walked to the deck to relax, think, and drink. I begin to look at all the things in my life that weren't going my way. This was a bad idea because I noticed that I began to see only the bad side of everything. I begin to think about my book. *Man, I'm not done yet. I just can't see how it will ever be completed. I'm not even where I want to be in life. I should have been further by now. Man, I should have never gotten married. I don't think he's the right one. I should have been further in ministry by now. I can't believe what people at church said to me.* In the middle of all that, one of my children called me. I thought, *See, I don't even have the freedom to think. I had my children at the wrong time by the wrong man. We moved to the wrong community. What have I done?* You see where this is going, right?

As a result, my whole day was ruined. I went to sleep with a little attitude. The very next day, I woke up, brushed my teeth, and ran down the stairs to make my nice cup of coffee. I'm a coffee drinker, so I can somehow determine how my day will go based on how good my coffee is. I'm sure that some of you can relate. My coffee was delicious just like the day before, so I headed to the deck to relax, think, and drink. I wasn't working at the time because I was on maternity leave. There I was, sitting on the deck, and I begin to think again. *Man, what am I going to do? I used all of my 401K money. I should have been further than this in life. I don't know what's going on with my family. I wish they would do better. What's wrong with them?*

Suddenly the Holy Spirit said, "Are you going to replay all those negative thoughts in your head again today? You did that yesterday, and as a result, your entire day was gloom and doom!"

I said, "It sure was."

The Holy Spirit said, "Have you noticed that whenever you start to think about everything that's wrong or off track in your life, your mood and environment shifts? That ruins your entire day."

I agreed. "It surely does." The Holy Spirit then led me to Philippians 4:8. "Finally, brethren, whatsoever things are true, whatsoever things are honest, whatsoever things are just, whatsoever things are pure, whatsoever things are lovely, whatsoever things are of good report; if there be any virtue, and if there be any praise, think on these things."

It was like a light bulb popped on. I said, "Not today, devil! I refuse to think about what went wrong. I will focus on what's right in my life." I begin to look at the fact that my eighth grader just graduated and had earned a valedictorian award. I thought about how my son also never missed a single day of school from pre pre-k until eighth grade. I remembered the blessing of the newest addition to our family and how all our other children were all healthy, happy, and whole. I considered that not every woman can have children, but God had blessed me to be very fruitful. I reminded myself that we didn't have just one home, but we now have two. As soon as I switched my thought process from negative to positive, I began to feel better with a great sense of energy, unlike the day before. Do you see how our thoughts can manipulate our feelings, and our feelings can ruin our day? So I challenge you, the next time you start to feeling down about your life, don't go there. It's a distraction to ruin your day. Do me a favor and remember what I'm telling you here today. I dare you to try it. You will see. Think only good thoughts, and you will experience better days.

Think of it this way. When a child is born, it's so innocent and pure with no spots or blemishes. It's so naive and so trusting, but then the hardness of man soon changed the condition of the heart of the child. But God still wants you to have a tender heart. I know you are probably questioning me, thinking, "Please, I'm no fool. I'll never be that naive again." I'm not speaking of being naive, but what I am speaking of is developing that childlike faith again. The bible talks about childlike faith that will not make you naïve. But this faith provides us with the ability to get rid of all the baggage, all the hurt, and all the pain of your past. It helps you with the ability to not take everything so personally and to not be so easily offended. The truth of the matter is, if you are going to emerge as an overcomer, then you must learn to wear everything and everyone as a loose garment. Did you ever see kids fight only to start playing together again a few minutes later? But adults aren't like that. The older we get, the more impossible it seems for us to let it go and to get back to having fun. We've become too entangled and ensnared by the cares of this world; we're too overly sensitive.

People will sometimes do things to hurt us, and the sooner we learn to let go, the sooner we can recover from the hurt. We can get back to being ourselves, the real us with that childlike faith. It will take faith to allow the real you to show up. When we allow the real us to show up, we can then stop acting like phonies and stop showing fake love to people, including ourselves. Being real allows you to be you. It's okay to just accept the fact that people will sometimes let you down, hurt you, or disappoint you.

Here's an example of what I mean. I was on the expressway here in Chicago today when a man in a huge pickup suddenly shifted over into my lane and almost caused a collision, scaring the daylights out of me. The old me would have been so upset. The real me said, "Oh, I don't think he saw me. He didn't even seem to know that he almost caused a collision." You get my point. In this life, we are traveling on a road. Sometimes people will mistakenly cross you. They don't have the slightest idea of how they made you feel. What I'm saying is that you should not take anything that people say or do so personally. Chances are that they can't really see you. More importantly, you don't have time to add even another ounce of frustration to your life.

Will the real you please stand up? By now, I'm sure you're asking yourself what it means to be the real you and wondering how you stand up. You must get rid of all that excess baggage, the years of hurt and pain. Some people don't even realize they hurt you while others might think that you're overly sensitive. The last group refuses to acknowledge that they did anything wrong at all. As I mentioned earlier, I had to learn the strategy of forgiveness at age twenty-nine from Dr. Wesley, my former employer.

How Did I Get Here?

Be careful of how you treat others. We must learn how to treat others the right way. Our behavior has a significant impact on the outcome and actions of others. This is the law of cause and effect. The way we treat others can determine what the person does next. And somehow our actions can change the outcome of someone else's life. I decided to answer the call of ministry that the Lord had been asking me to step into for years. I finally said yes. I was working as a store manager with little or no time to fully answer God's call to ministry. On top of that, I had to work tremendously hard to untangle myself from all the pain associated with my past. I was focusing on not drinking or smoking cigarettes. I was working on the poor self-image that the enemy and the world tried to put on me. I was finally free from all those things except one: smoking cigarettes. My brother-in-law asked me to become his assistant pastor, and everyone in my family seemed to have a problem with that. I thought, *Wow, when I was drunk and in the world, people seemed okay with that. And now that I have accepted the call of God on my life, ya'll church folk have a problem with that.* Their actions hurt me so badly. Here I found myself in a hard place again. I didn't know that doing good and living for God was so widely unaccepted. This hurt me to my core.

So I found myself wandering for years after this all happened. Shortly after this, I wound up marrying an unsaved guy. In my opinion, that marriage was from hell. Looking back, I think I was just looking for someone to love me since those around me did not. In my mind, he was the one showing love—albeit fake love—to me. This relationship took me for the worse turn that I'd ever experienced in my adult life. This man treated me in such a degrading manner. He tried to hit on my niece. I often asked myself, "How in the world did I get here?" Today I looked back, and the Lord began to answer those questions. I married this man because I was in a season in my life where I needed someone to love me. After all, my family didn't know how. My mom's husband gave me a music CD that said that he saw the best in me when everyone around me could only see the worst in me. That song was just how I felt about my new husband. I was now at a time when I couldn't believe my own family wouldn't accept my call to ministry. I became spiritually vulnerable to falling into a relationship and then marrying the wrong guy. On top of that, we started to have kids.

Thoughts on the LGBTQ Issue

There's a lot of talk surrounding the area of transgendered brothers and sisters. I thank God for giving me the capacity to love and embrace all his people. One day, I hugged a transgendered woman; she was so loving and compassionate, a very kind person. The Lord wants us to love people from all walks of life. The goal is to love them back to health, happiness, and wholeness. Can you imagine the pain that some people might have had to endure? Think of all the torment that they might have had to experience in coming out of the closet, in making a decision to go ahead and get the surgery that would make them feel more comfortable. Imagine the name-calling they might have had to endure, the wrong looks, and negative slurs that people who lacked love might have made toward them. My point here is that everyone deserves love, not judgment. In fact, 1 Corinthians 4:5 says that we should judge nothing before its time. See, I too have been misjudged by others because no one ever stopped to show concern by asking if I was alright. Who knows what may have led individuals down the road that they decided to take? Were they too mistreated; were they abused? Who am I to put more pressure on them? My role is to love them unconditionally and to embrace them, care for them, and pray for them just as I would do for anyone else. We have to learn the *agape* love of god covers all. In fact, Proverbs 10:12 states that love covers a multitude of faults. So even if I'm wrong, you should love me enough to overlook what I look like and see me as the person I am and the person I long to be. Everyone needs love. Love provides strength, courage, and the opportunity to hope again and face another day. As the people of God, we are to be the light of the world, loving enough to share the *agape* love of God with all of mankind.

Love Yourself

I addressed this topic in another chapter but want to take another look at it here. One of the greatest gifts that one could receive is the gift of salvation, a personal relationship with God. This is more than just being a church goer; it's an intimate connection with God. It's awesome because it allows God to really minister to our hearts and minds. It's a place of prayer. Not a quick prayer we pray, but a time that we take out of our busy day just to acknowledge him as God. I'm so glad I found what we church folk call that secret place—a place in God he wants to get us to where the cares of this world become irrelevant. A place where we pray, and God hears, and then we listen for him to speak to our hearts. The truth is that giving my life to the Lord allowed me to find my life and regain my true identity in him. I was broken because of all the traumatic experiences I faced in life, but through my personal relationship with God, he turned around the whole situation. He began to teach me in his Word that he loves me, and he loves me unconditionally. He showed me that I am fearfully and wonderfully made. (See Psalm 139.) He informed me that, in spite of what I've had to suffer, he still has me in the palm of his hands. And though I might have to suffer for a little while because of the evil in this present world, at the end of the story, he's given me everything I needed to be successful. He's given me beauty for ashes.

He showed me that if I would just trust him, then he had the power to pull the brokenness of my heart back together again. He showed me how to love and how to forgive. He explained why these things happened and why I must forgive so that I will not be held hostage by the weapons of the enemy. He taught me that he didn't want any evil emotions hanging over my head. He told me in his Word that he paid the price for the cost of my freedom when Jesus died on the cross. And I tell you that the Lord wants you to be free as well. John 8:36 says that whom the Son sets free is free indeed. He walked me through years of anger, hurt, bitterness, confusion, and hardness of heart and gave me peace.

2 Timothy 2:3-5 says that "thou therefore endure hardness, as a good soldier of Jesus Christ. No man that warreth entangleth himself with the affairs of this life; that he may please him who hath chosen him to be a soldier. And if a man also strive for masteries, yet is he not crowned, except he strive lawfully." In this life, we might face many hard trials, but we must remain strong like a soldier, not easily offended or trapped in bitterness because that can lead us to sin.

It's Not the Kids

When children walk in error, it means that something is going on around them that's not correct at home. I don't want to hurt your feelings, but the truth only stings for a little while and like alcohol will keep infections away. Parents, you drive your own children to the streets by not establishing a proper foundation. Now I'm not here to hurt you, but you need to understand that the enemy starts to pull our children into a world of trouble at an early age. And we have to learn to be aware of that enemy by laying a solid foundation so that we can break the cycles from this foolishness and not pass them on to the next generation. Don't get me wrong, you can pretend all you want. But the truth will set you and your entire family free. (See John 8:32.) Lay a proper foundation. Do things the right way so that you're not sorry later.

Believe me, I had to explain the same things that I'm telling you here to the judge when my twenty-seven-year-old son was facing thirty years in prison. I had to explain to the judge what horrible circumstances led my child to prison. Life has a domino effect. What affects me affects others; what affects me in my childhood will also affect my children. I had to get real and take responsibility for the role I ignorantly played in his life. Even though I was an adult, I wasn't healed; the fact that I was a grown-up didn't make me change. Psalm 11:3 says that if the foundations be destroyed, what will the righteous do? Children come into this world as innocent; we damage them through our ignorance and the absence of a loving God. I see why Psalm 111:10 says that the fear of the Lord is the beginning of wisdom. If we don't have wisdom, we will continue to raise our children up in unhealthy environments. I'm not speaking in terms of religion, but I'm talking about having a genuine relationship with the Creator, a God that we seek daily.

Men, I'm speaking to you first. It all starts with you; you are the head of the family and must take your rightful place. We have to come to a place, people of God, when only God leads and guides us. In the body dwells no good thing. (See Romans 7, especially verse 18.) God expects us to provide the best for our families. He's given us families to love, nurture, and care for one another. Love is sacrifice. The greatest expression of love is self-sacrifice. The only reason that people can't love must be because they are not a real human.

God's Mandate

Does anyone love the Lord? I'm sure many of you would say that you do with your hands raised high. That's great. We all have the shirt on that says, "I love God so much!" But we struggle with loving your neighbors as yourself. (See John 13:34.) And we need to fulfill that mandate as well. Everyone seems to be looking to fulfill their kingdom mandate and their kingdom assignments. But a shift is coming to the Body of Christ to follow God's real mandate—the mandate to love. People in life seek all sorts of platforms to fulfill a call, but this mandate is for the world, the mandate to love.

Everyone Wants to Win

Everyone wants to be successful in the inner city, including those who most would consider a total loss. Most people in the ghettos, housing projects, or even low-income areas wear very nice clothing. From the nails to the hair, their swag is top notch. We purchase the most expensive shoes, the latest styles and trends. We don't mind spending money on our children so that they look good. I worked in the community as a Medicaid sales consultant. I came across a young lady who, of course, was on Medicaid. Shortly after I assisted her with enrollment into a free health plan, I asked her, "So where are you off to now?"

She said, "Girl, I'm about to go buy my one-year-old some True Religion jeans."

I said, "That's nice."

She said, "Yeah, I know, they cost me $250.00."

I replied, "Really." I thought to myself, *Wow, I know she really loves her son. But that money could be used to send him to college.* See, I'm from the hood, so I totally understand that we go all out for our children, sometimes unnecessarily trying to make up for the areas in which we lack. We go above and beyond in providing for our kids because we truly know that what we really have to offer is not enough.

We lack solid support systems probably because we have not been trained. I seriously believe that the difference between the *haves* and the *have nots* is the right information. So we live life with these fake traditions and errors handed down to us from generation to generation. We've learned to value things instead of people. Mark 8:36 says, "For what shall it profit a man, if he shall gain the whole world, and lose his own soul?" In some communities, we express love through how much we spend and how much we give. What we need to do instead is to offer our time and attention to building relationships and solidifying them.

My point is this: no one in life choses to be unsuccessful. No one choses to be bad, and no one sets out to become a career criminal. Misinformation and miseducation is the primary reason that many of the individuals in our communities are unsuccessful.

As I previously mentioned, the Bible says if the foundations be destroyed, what will the righteous do? In most homes, the foundation was pretty rocky one. So now you have communities of people that are living life with either a broken foundation or with no foundation at all. No foundation means that everything was set up wrong from the very beginning. We have men who were designed by God to be the head of the home, yet they are absent from the home, leaving the women and children in vulnerable positions. Why? Because their foundation was destroyed at some point. Most men in communities where I come from were not all bad; they just received little or no training. They were misinformed in the training they did receive. But thank God, it all begins with one man deciding to do the right thing by honoring God. The rest will then fall into place.

When there was no king in Israel, every man did what was right in his own eyes, according to Judges 21:25. The inner city lacks strong leadership, hands-on leadership that the community can connect with, those who talk the talk and walk the walk. This connection, this sense of similarity, is critical in order to grasp the attention of the inner city youth and parents alike. We need the sort of leadership that has not forgotten what it means to be without, what it means to have hope and dreams and information that will cause an individual to rise from their current mind set.

Even in the church, the blood of the saints is being shed. I'm not talking about the blood of Jesus or holy communion. Many lives are lost in the streets, and the blood being shed is partly because the church is taking too long to cast out all fear. You can't operate in love until you allow the Holy One of Israel to cast out all fear. As the Body of Christ, we need love, the *agape* kind of love, not that Sunday-morning, fake-saint love. We need the unconditional love of God to shed abroad in our hearts so that this same love will began to spill over into our homes, spill over into our communities, and then spill over into the cities and to the nations and to the uttermost parts of the world.

Our young people in the streets are only there because they too are looking for love, so they team up with people in the community that accept them just the way they are. They join gangs and become loyal to that gang because that's who shows them love. But this so-called love does not lead to a life of abundance and happiness like God promises us in his Word. God's Word says I come that you might have life and life more abundantly. (See John 10:10.)

I don't know about you, but I laugh at people when they look down on young folk with shame and disgrace as if they were never young and they forgot their own actions. It didn't make sense when they did it either. Yes, we know that God has thrown all of our sins into the sea to remember them no more, but as the people of God we must never forget how far the Lord has brought us and how merciful God has been to us. (See Micah 7:19.) We should never shut our doors and become afraid to reach out to help, nurture, and love our young people. I don't know about you personally, but in my lifetime, I have done some dumb things. Later on in life, I looked back and said, "What was I thinking? Why would I do something so foolish?" Of course, I wouldn't do those things today. That's why 1 Corinthians 13: 11 says, "When I was a child, I spake as a child, I understood as a child, I thought as a child: but when I became a man, I put away childish things." And that's exactly what we as the Body of Christ need to do. It's time to put away all those childish ways, cast out all fear, and love the way that God has designed us to love.

Just think of how much peace would be on the earth, in our homes, communities, and on our jobs. Imagine your workplace full of real smiles, happiness, and cheer. As a young lady going to work with women, oh, my God, cat fights seemed to be going on all throughout the day. In most cases, those cat fights were the result of fear—fear that someone might be more talented or desirable than you. I often heard female co-workers say that they didn't want to train anyone because the person was always promoted over them.

As a young woman in corporate America, I had been through pure hell. I was thankful and grateful just for the opportunity to have a job, let alone a career. I showed up happy, but for how long? People without love will try to knock the wind right out of your sails. I didn't know that every smiling face was not genuine. Before I learned better, I used to think that it was me. I wondered why there were always problems wherever I showed up to work.

At one point, I experienced a lot of harshness at work. I came in as an assistant to an African-American woman. I thought, *She would love to train me, teach me the ropes, be my mentor, guide me, and provide me with the tools I need to be a success in the store. She will instill some values in me that I can put into practice for the rest of my life.* But she did just the opposite, and I couldn't understand why. I was more than just a pretty face. I came to work early, stayed late, dropped in on my off days just to say *hi* and to lend a helping hand. I thought she would have sensed my passion and the fact that I was hungry for knowledge. I thought that she would take time teach me and train me, but she didn't. She only taught me the basics of opening and closing. She was never interested in investing in me. I felt so frustrated, so I asked her when we could spend some training time together.

She just looked at me and said, "There's no time." The staff became very upset whenever they learned that I was the manager they would have to close with. The staff under me was so very disrespectful and pushed back on me often. I had a feeling that she was saying hateful things about me and stirring up problems. I later received confirmation of this.

One day, I was scheduled for closing with a certain store associate, so I geared up for the night. I got thirsty and decided to purchase a drink and snack for the associate on my shift. When I handed this young lady the drink and snack, she began to cry. She said, "Talicia, I'm so sorry for how I've treated you. I only treated you that way because of what they were saying." My manager was there as she was crying, and the manager was frowning. The young lady then looked at my manager and told her, "We need to have a meeting." With tears in her eyes, she told me, "Talicia, you are so kind, and you're a hard worker. You're good at what you do, and I like you. I don't have a problem with you." She looked back at my manager and asked again, "Can we have a meeting?"

My manager rolled her eyes and said, "Girl, I'm about to go home," and backed out the door. The next time I was scheduled to work with that same associate, she didn't show up, and I never saw her again. I asked my manager about her a couple of times. She lied and told me that she quit because she couldn't read or pass the exams.

I winked my eye at the wall and said, "Okay." I continued to be faithful there in my work. I wasn't mad, and I didn't have an attitude even knowing that this manager was the cause of all of this frustration. I continued to do above and beyond what was expected of me. Within six months, that manager was fired from the company after being there for nineteen years. I did not sabotage her job. Her own fear fired her.

How many times have we found ourselves on our knees or in a situation where we needed a change, a break, or some help? For those of you who pray, you prayed, and others did whatever they could to ask for help. Then when God sends us the help, we forgot we prayed. We're quick to pull out a sword and kill the help that we cried out to God for. Why did we kill the help? Because we didn't recognize it when we saw it. It wasn't packaged the way we thought it should have been. That's why 1 John 4:18 says, "perfect love casts out fear." Wouldn't it be nice to recognize what is sent by God as opposed to what is not? We never know, which is why we must operate in love at all times, casting down fear and every vain imagination. We don't want to mistake a friend for a foe and crucify what God intended to deliver us with.

This doesn't just happen in the work force. It happens at church more often than it should. How are saints killing one another in the church? They then have the nerve to talk about how much killing and murders and bloodshed is happening in communities all across America. The reason for all the calamity is because of the enemy. His goal is to rob our love. Love is our prized possession because it's everything we need to be whole and to be free.

Did you know that everything grows with love? Life looks better with love. When we give or receive love, our brain produces dopamine, a chemical that helps control the reward and the pleasure center in the brain.[16]

If you were anything like me—hurt broken, angry, bitter, enraged, hot-tempered—you too would laugh at the scripture that says to turn the other cheek or love those that mistreat you and be kind to those that persecute you. (See Matthew 5:38-40.) I used to be a very vengeful and vindictive person. If you ever crossed me, I wanted to make sure you paid for it, either with your life or for the rest of your life. If you messed with me, that was it. I didn't want to stop until I saw blood. I used to be so angry. I couldn't imagine obeying those scriptures.

Once, my sister came to my house. She was drunk and upset because she

---

[16] Scott Edwards, "Love and the Brain," *Harvard Mahoney Neuroscience Institute,* Accessed February 25, 2018, http://neuro.hms.harvard.edu/harvard-mahoney-neuroscience-institute/brain-newsletter/and-brain-series/love-and-brain.

lost a couple of leather jackets that I lent to her and her friend to wear to this party. She kept dodging me about these jackets. On this night, she was drunk and decided to come screaming and yelling to my window because she was mad at me because I was mad at her for losing my jackets. She couldn't face me sober, so she decided to wait until she was drunk. As soon as I heard her, I told myself that she was drunk. I wasn't looking for trouble, so I tried as long as possible to ignore her. I turned up the TV and went to the back of the house, which wasn't that big. She was just cussing and calling me all kinds of ungodly names. She must have been there for at least thirty minutes. Finally, I couldn't tune her out any longer. I opened the window and asked her twice to please get away from my window. Now my sister was like me with anger issues. She was known in the community for slicing and dicing peoples' skin.

So I closed the window for what I hoped was the last time and tried to ignore her again. I wasn't scared of her. I just understood all that we'd been through as children. I was mostly sober and thought, *I will try to be the sensible one today.*

But then I heard my sister shout, "You think you're pretty. I will cut your face up."

Her threat rubbed me the wrong way. That was it. I jumped up in my shorts, threw on a blouse, and headed for the door. At the time, I probably weighed about 110 pounds, and she probably weighed 180 pounds. I decided that I was going to make her move from my front door. Her threat to cut me hurt me the most. I had already been rejected by many people because of the way I looked, and to find that my sister was carrying that in her heart was unbearable for me. I couldn't believe that she wanted to hurt me. We started fighting from my house to momma's house, which was across the street. We were in her kitchen, and she still wanted to fight me. Now she was mad at me because she lost my coats and never said anything to me about it. She spotted a knife on the table. She reached for it, but I grabbed it first. I could see in her face that wanted to hurt me, so I cut the top of her arm. I couldn't believe that I did that and was so upset. I told her, "See, I begged you to leave me alone, didn't I? I begged you."

She still wanted to fight some more. That was the day I said to myself that my sister was just like everyone else, and she really wanted to hurt me. So I took her to the ER and had the doctors patch her up.

This gives you an idea of what I thought when I heard the expression, "turn the other cheek." I thought, *Who, me? Please, I'm grown now, and I will not allow anyone to ever hurt me again.* I definitely refused to turn the other cheek. Today I understand how to turn the other cheek. I knew I was really saved and filled with the love of God when a niece of mine brushed up against me, and I didn't say a word. People did a lot of little things to pick at me, but I ignored them.

God trained me to not say anything. I understood that it wasn't about me, and as long as I stood and did what was right, then things would eventually go my way. I learned this lesson after years of God humbling me. When I worked as an assistant store manager. I was so happy to have this job. Some thought the job and the company was a small thing, but I had my own business for years. Closing it down didn't seem small to me.

It's not about You

As you can see, I had a lot of negative baggage in my life, so when I write this book, I'm writing from a very personal place of experience. In life, we must understand that the love God desires us to display is not about us but about the people around us. Their love will be about you. A lack of love drives people away, and in most cases, causes them to go into unlikely places they'd never imagined they would go. A lack of love will cause you to seek out love in all the wrong places just as I did when I dated that big-time drug dealer at seventeen. But you know my story and where that got me—in a huge mess.

The one thing that I did know about drugs was that Daddy said not to ever use them, or I'd wind up like a formerly beautiful role model that I'd admired around my grandmother's house. This lady was fly to me. She'd worked for the state and had her own two-flat building. She looked sharp as a tack every day with her swag on point—her shoes matched her purse. *Suited and booted* is what we called it. She was a very professional young woman. But I started to see her appearance go from being a hero to a zero. That's when Daddy had the talk with me about drugs and why not to do them.

1 Corinthians 15:33 says that evil communications corrupt good manners. Yes, the Bible was right. But something happened when I saw one of my classmates in the drug line, and it broke my heart. I saw what

these drugs did to people. I made my way in the house, and I was so high, but I prayed to God, "Lord, please forgive me. I don't know how I got to this point, but please don't leave me right here." I woke up the next day, looked at myself in the mirror and didn't like what I saw.

It still took me two years. I was nineteen and living with him, and my life was spinning in this downward spiral after seeing what drugs did to him. I made up my mind to never do that junk again because I saw the change in my face. I prayed to God and got out of that relationship one night after he beat me up for the bill money. I didn't get strung out because I stopped going where they would go. I still had to spend time in jail, but God delivered me.

Learning to Endure

In this life, you will have to endure hardships, but you must forgive.

While I do not believe these negative emotions help you, I totally understand why people become stuck. You can easily fall into the slump of becoming angry or bitter over circumstances—circumstances that you might not have even caused that were primarily due to the actions or inactions of another. In life, we should control what we can control, and not worry about the rest. But I beg to differ because now I was left to deal a hand that I had no dealings in. I didn't even ask to be a part of these charades. If we really want to know the truth, most of this foolishness was created long before we were even conceived. I remember asking, "God, if life was going to be like this, why was I even born?" This sounds a lot like what Job said in the Bible. In fact, things became so bad for Job that he cursed the day he was born. (See Job 3:1.) I've been through so many challenges until I asked the Lord, "What did I ever do to you?"

Life can feel like hell sometimes, especially when those who were designed to love you wound you instead. I went through life feeling as if everyone I decided to love ended up hurting or disappointing me. I often wondered how you could love someone and then hurt them. How could you destroy what God has given you to love? But everyone has their cross to bear. My argument is with Hosea 4:6 that says that people perish due to a lack of knowledge. I genuinely believe that if people understood the power and benefits of love, they'd never violate the love laws. I believe if mankind was fully aware of the damage that was done from a lack of love, he would see life a whole lot differently. We'd treat and respond to one another differently. We'd be very careful about what we say or do to others.

I want readers to understand that a real evil force out here is working against us and is contrary to the plans and purposes of God. This evil force, Satan and his angels, has been on assignment since the beginning of time. Satan's ultimate assignment is to rid the hearts and minds of mankind of love. Since love is the only force that can defeat Satan, he's been on the rampage to defy God and deprive mankind of the love of God because God is love. That's why the enemy has been at work to destroy you ever since you can remember—for some of you, even before you were born. Satan wants to destroy the love of God in our hearts.

No wonder Genesis 50:20 says that, what the enemy meant for your evil, I will make it for your good. Joseph's brothers hated him because he was a dreamer. They hated him so much that they plotted to murder him; however, they instead decided to put him into a pit and then later sold their own blood into slavery. Not only was Joseph a dreamer, he also walked in the divine favor of God on his life. This favor was at work throughout the life of Joseph and caused him to rise even as a slave and be promoted to the top wherever he would go. No matter how difficult his life was as a slave to his boss, the Pharaoh, the favor of the almighty God superimposed the plans and purposes of Satan. Poor Joseph was even falsely accused of trying to rape the Pharaoh's wife. Though falsely accused and thrown into prison, the favor of God eventually brought him out of the trap of prison, and he was set free and placed second-in-command next to Pharaoh.

Although the scriptures don't mention it, as a human with emotions, I believe that God allowed Joseph to sit in that prison for thirteen years so that he could properly deal with the matters of his heart. He must have had many struggles in his mind about his circumstances: what his brothers had done to him, taking him from life as he knew it, selling him, attempting to kill him, and how he was left sitting in jail because of his own blood brothers. Imagine how he must have felt after having to endure all of that pain. Yet when the time came, God allowed Joseph's brothers to be placed in a situation where they needed him. God knew Joseph would handle this correctly because of all that he had endured. Despite the fact that Joseph's brothers betrayed him and tried to kill him, yet God turned around the situation and put their survival in his hands.

That's when the dreams of Joseph's youth came to pass.

That's why we need a relationship with God so that our love stays intact. Without the love of God, we're capable and apt to do just about anything. As I stated before, just as the Trinity: the Father, Son, and Holy Spirit, is three parts, so we too are tri-part beings. We are a spirit; we have a soul, and we live in this body. Each part of our being has a specific function. Our spirit is our God-consciousness or the part that without a doubt recognizes there is a God. Our spirit also always seeks to do good and seeks the will of God. Secondly, our soul is where our mind, will, and emotions are housed. This is also known as self-consciousness. Our feelings are based in the heart, such as: I like him; I don't like her; I can do anything, or no, I can't do it. Our emotions live here. You cry, you laugh; you're sad. All of these come from your soul. Thirdly, we have our body, which is our sense-consciousness—touch, taste, see, hear, and smell. These three are known as our tri-part.

God intended for mankind to be led by the Spirit of God. Galatians 5:16 tells us to walk in the Spirit, and we won't fulfill the lusts (cravings, desires) of the flesh (body, soul) (feelings, senses). Romans 8:14 says that those who are led by the Spirit of God are the sons of God. This means that God intended for the spirit of man to be bigger, stronger, and more powerful than his soul and body when we have a personal relationship with God and when we're spending time in prayer, reading the Word of God daily and attending church regularly. When we do these things, we're building spiritual muscle. That's right. We're getting a much-needed spiritual work out in. We need it because our soul and body double-teams the spirit.

Let me explain. Have you ever thought about doing something wrong, and then suddenly you hear a small voice tell you not to do that; it's not right? That's the tri-part in operation. You remember seeing cartoons when the devil was on one shoulder, an angel on the other, and you're in the middle. Why is it that every time I seek to do good, evil is always present? (See Romans 7:21.) That's your mind and body that are at war with your spirit. If your sprit is weak, mankind will sink to the lowest state of his being. That's why the Bible says, "For the word of God is quick, and powerful, and sharper than any two-edged sword, piercing even to the dividing asunder of soul and spirit, and of the joints and marrow, and is a discerner of the thoughts and intents of the heart" (Hebrew 4:12). So what I'm telling you is that we need love, but love without God is sometimes wishy-washy. Life without God is a life without the full expression of God's plan for love. You are probably all too familiar with the term, "The devil made me do it." Have you ever loved someone, but your actions expressed the total opposite? Satan will use anyone who's not filled with the Holy Spirit to commit his acts of offense, murder, slander, strife, confusion, incest, rape, child molestation, witchcraft, adultery, fornication, theft, suicide, mass murder, and more. For every action, there's a reaction—a response, the purpose of which is to ignite hate in the hearts of those who fall victim. Then he works to destroy the perpetrator by placing them in bondage of guilt, shame, isolation, hurt, blame, and other negative emotions.

The only way to defeat this evil is to submit our lives to God because he is love, and love is the only force that will defeat every evil work. Love is cure. According to 1 Corinthians 13, love is patient and kind; love never fails; it does not envy or boast; love counts no wrongs. Everything grows with love because love is cure.

This love I speak of is difficult to find and is not obtained simply because you're a good person or due to the fact that you're a Christian, Catholic, Muslim, or a church goer. This love is only established through a personal relationship with God and the indwelling of the Holy Spirit. Without the love of God and the Holy Spirit, there's no telling what might happen.

More than a Conqueror

"Nay, in all these things we are more than conquers through him that loved us" (Romans 8:37). Yes, God's love for us has the power to turn every situation for our good and turn our sorrow into pure joy. God uses the pain of our past to promote us. As sons and daughters of the Most High God, all we need to do is receive the love of God. The love of God is unconditional love, that sacrificial love that Jesus offered up to redeem mankind from the very clutches of the evil one. In this life, there will be some pain. But we have the power to push past the pain, hurt, bitterness, betrayal, and disappointment. We must push past the fact that others might not have any idea how to love. Without the love of God, there's no way for others to love you. No wonder King Solomon wrote in Proverbs 9:10, "The fear of the Lord is the beginning of wisdom: and the knowledge of the holy is understanding."

These days, our prayer should be, "Father, teach us how to love God's way. Remove all bitterness and anger from our hearts. Don't allow our hearts to become callous because of this world's system or the way the world decides to live. Bless us so that we are not affected by the evil one, but keep us in perfect peace so that our minds are stayed on you." (See Isaiah 26:3.)

With all that's going on in the world today, this book is intended to encourage you to be of good cheer and to love in spite of how cold this world might appear to be. As Romans 5:5 tells us, "Let the love of God be shed abroad in our hearts," no matter what's happening in our world. Despite what goes on in our personal lives, the events in the world are beyond our control because as I referenced already, in all these things, we are more than conquerors. God loves us so much that he calls us "friend." Because God loves us, his Word even says in 1 John 4:4 that greater is he who is in you than he that is in the world. My friend, I cannot begin to tell you how many times the love of God has lifted me. God's love has kept me, shielded me, and protected me. God cares for us.

God loves us so much. I realize that many challenges I faced were bad. The conditions were bad too, but they could have been worst. I could have been dead. God didn't have to allow the Holy Spirit to warn me. If the Holy Spirit had not warned me in some of these situations, and if I had not followed his prompting, I wouldn't be here to write this book. I wouldn't be here to tell you these things. Despite all the people against you—who didn't love you, who didn't do right by you, who let you down, who betrayed you or disappointed you—you are still more than a conqueror in Christ Jesus. Thank God we weren't wiped out because our story is not over and will not end here. 2 Corinthians 5:17 tells us that the former things are passed away, and we have a bigger, brighter future to look forward to.

The Most Powerful Force on Earth Is Love

The most powerful force on earth is love, the weapon of mass destruction. Love affects our entire being: our body, soul, and spirit. In order to fulfill God's mandate to love, we must seek after the things of God. Matthew 6:33 says to seek first the kingdom of God and his righteousness, and then all the other things shall be added unto us. Therefore, we must put our spirit man in charge, and in order to do that, we must be born again. Romans 8:14 says that those that are led by the Spirit of God are the sons of God. God's intentional plan for man was that we be led by his Spirit so that the spirit man rules our entire body, soul, and spirit.

Have you ever had a negative thought, suggesting something that was morally incorrect, and then the next thought that popped in your mind was not to do that? God intended for our spirit man to rule us; however, an inner and outer struggle for power is going on in man. Our spirit must receive the Word of God daily, just like we need to work out daily. Then we will walk in the Spirit, and we won't fulfill the lust of the flesh or the soul: the mind, will, and emotions. When we don't fill up with truth, which is the Word of God, we become open and vulnerable to Satan's suggestions. That's why we see people commit all sorts of crimes and offenses against one another. They have no spiritual prayer life and no time to spend with God, either. Proverbs 4:7 tells us, "Wisdom is the principal thing; therefore get wisdom: and with all thy getting get understanding." The enemy knows that if we are to ever get this love thing down pat, no one would be available to cause havoc for him or to do his evil bidding. Lives would no longer be destroyed. If you think that a loveless life is good, then you lack knowledge. People are destroyed due to a lack of knowledge.

I often wonder what the world would be like if we were ever in one accord and if we ever experienced that real kind of *agape* love. This would be heaven on earth. Many people around the world say, "I can't wait to get to heaven."

I say, "Why wait? We can produce heaven right here on earth." I imagine if we have God's love, wars and selfishness would cease. No one would grow hungry, and they would have no need to cheat or deprive others. I believe this is the place that God wants to get mankind to. Jesus Christ has already paid the price for us. Man's selfish desires would be under control. I know you're probably thinking that this would be possible in a perfect world, but you are saying that we don't live in a perfect world. But let's just start with you. "Let your light so shine before men, that they may see your good works, and glorify your Father which is in heaven" (Matthew 5:16).

I know some might argue that doing wrong feels good and that hurting people feels good to them. And to them, I say, "There is still hope for you. God loves you too." Some might argue that if they love, they won't have power. I would say that if you don't have a real relationship with God, then you are powerless anyway. Some might say that they feel joy when they do the innocent wrong. I say, "You don't know real joy until you have had a divine encounter with God." Some might argue that God is a bunch of fairytales. But I will tell them about my friend who saw death and told me two weeks before he was killed, as I shared about earlier in this book. Some might say that God is for the illiterate. I say that the love of God is for everyone.

My point is that there's more to gain in love than living without love. I'm not talking about fake love; I'm talking about the true *agape* unconditional love of God, a love that seeks to protect, do what's right, and not violate other human beings. I feel sorry for anyone that doesn't accept the fact that love is cure. If we love well, we'll live well. I know you might think that if I love, I will lose. I tell you that I have nothing to lose and everything to gain. The people around you would be happier, and you'd be happier and live your life with a sense of fulfillment. My point to you is, don't deny love. Because love is cure!

Never Underestimate the Consequences

Let's be clear here. Whether or not we realize it, every decision we make and every step we take has the ability to positively or negatively affect others. Therefore, we mustn't take how we live lightly because our decisions have the capacity not only to affect our lives but the world around us as well. That why the Bible clearly states in Deuteronomy 30:19 that "I call heaven and earth to record this day against you, that I have set before you life and death, blessing and cursing: therefore choose life, that both thou and thy seed may live." This life is not all about you, but we are all interconnected. That's why God instructs us to love. When one man kills another, it has the power and capacity to not only negatively affect his life, but his family: mom and dad, sisters and brothers, and more importantly, the lives of his children. It's no wonder the Bible instructs us to love one another. People, I firmly believe that if we would have done things God's way in the first place, we would not have ended up in a bad position.

Can we just be real? Whenever a person decides to pursue their own selfish plans, it will end in disaster. Therefore we must want for others what we'd want for ourselves, in families, in society, and in all relationships. Stop wanting others to be subservient to you. Stop attempting to look down on them. Stop putting others down so that you can feel big. The truth of the matter is that only small-minded people make others feel small. Those who are truly big will only bring about the best in others.

That's why I never understood prejudice. I know it was all about money. But how could I sleep at night, knowing that I caused another person pain, fear, or hate? I cannot allow hate to consume my life. That's why people are on drugs and pain killers, trying to numb themselves from the reality of doing wrong to others. They can't take it, so they can't stay sober long enough to feel human again. Who wants to be bound by hate and fear? Bondage is not of God. He said in Matthew 11:30, "For my yoke is easy, and my burden is light. Yet mankind chooses to stay in bondage even though God doesn't want us living in bondage. God came into this world not to condemn the world but that the world through Jesus Christ would be saved. (See John 3:17.) That means salvation and freedom for all. God comes to give us an abundant life. John 8:36 says, "if the Son therefore shall make you free, ye shall be free indeed." No matter who you are, no matter where you are, you must let love abound and allow the love of God to abound toward you more and more.

Love Is All About Relationship

It doesn't matter where we go in life, from Hammond, Indiana to Hollywood to New York City; we will find people in all walks of life with relational conflict. No matter how rich or how poor, we will find daughters who have issues with moms, sons with fathers, children with parents, husbands with wives. You get my point. The reason for all this conflict is that there is an attack against families. The enemy knows that there is power in numbers and power in unity. He wants to stop all relationships in the early stages.

The enemy knows that you're only as strong as your weakest link. The enemy's goal is to break up family unity early on in life before relationships have the time to grow and develop into something greater. He wants to see to it that no bond is created because the Bible states that a three-fold cord is not easily broken. (See Ecclesiastes 4:12.) The enemy understands the power of agreement. He knows that if you and your family ever stood together in unity, if husbands and wives ever joined in agreement, then communities would come together; nations would come together, and the world would come together. And that's a force to be reckoned with. So the enemy creates error, error in the house and error in the hearts and mind. He's strategic, so he does this early in life. All that calamity in your family is due to the fact that the enemy knows the power of love. In order to get you to forfeit your power and steal your love, he attempts to bring in misunderstanding, disagreement, and confusion.

In All Thy Getting, Get Understanding

Love is all about relationship. You need to understand and know that the people in your life are merely doing the best they can. No matter how messed up they seem, no matter how much they have messed up their own lives, causing problems in your life, it is what it is. You have to see that people have done the best they could from where they were in life. You don't wake up one day, knowing how to parent. Some people weren't even taught how to parent. God still has the power to preserve us despite how difficult people might have made our lives. I don't know about you, but I have made the decision to refuse to allow the enemy to keep me bound, tied, and chained to hurt, bitterness, anger, disappointment, and fear because someone didn't understand how to love me right. I refuse to allow the enemy to rob me of my time. I can't afford to dwell on the past because if I do, it will rob me of my future.

You now know that the devil comes to kill, steal, and destroy (John 10:10). He doesn't want you to even be free to love. He wants you trapped in the past—past hurts, past failures, and past disappointments. But I dare you to turn every area of your life where you've been hurt, wronged, or mistreated over to God and watch him turn that thing around for you. That stuff weighs you down. Let it go. God's Word says to cast your cares upon him because he cares for you. (See 1 Peter 5:7.) In life, we will suffer afflictions at different times, but 2 Corinthians 4:17 says that these light afflictions will not be compared to the glory of the Lord that shall be revealed through us (paraphrased). I'm not proud of the pain I previously endured. But one thing's for sure: I wouldn't have written this book had I not experienced what it was for Satan to steal your love away through error, offense, strife, misunderstanding, disagreement, and confusion. And I'm sure you can relate, at least in part. Why? Satan wants your love because God is love. When you have God, you have everything you need because God is love.

The Truth Will Set You Free

The Holy Spirit wants to set you free. That's why John 8:32 tells us that the truth comes to set us free. The truth is that you are not crazy and neither are your offenders, those you need to forgive. Some know exactly what occurred, and some do not. Jesus was on the cross and prayed, "Father, forgive them; for they know not what they do" (Luke 23:34a). This is an indication that some are unaware of their actions as a result of demonic possessions. I won't go into that at this point. But these people need deliverance and your prayers. You can do the following:

1. You have to understand that you must forgive people for their faults because God has forgiven you.

2. You must become unoffendable. In doing so, you will leave room for others to err, but their actions will have no impact on you, your emotions, or your reactions.

3. Train yourself to disregard what others think or how they feel about you. This will also cause you to become unoffended. Understand that we are human and are subject to error. We make mistakes and so do others.

4. Understand that it takes courage and power to admit a fault. It also takes great courage to forgive.

5. Remember that some might not understand life the way that you do. Their perception might be totally based on their reality. That's okay too. Life has many stages and phases, and some take just a little bit longer for the lights to come on. With this information, you have now become equipped with wisdom, patience, and the capacity to understand that some people are just not there yet.

6. You cannot afford to allow evil to contaminate your system (your spirit, soul, and body) or to occupy your energy, time, and space. I'm referring to contaminates such as strife, offense, and unforgiveness that can make you sick. If more people knew and understood this principle, a lot of sicknesses would be eliminated because love is cure!

We must give the Lord all our burdens. 2 Corinthians 10:4-6 tells us to cast down or throw down every imagination and every high thing that exalts itself against the knowledge of God. What is the knowledge of God? According to Proverbs 1:7, "the fear of the Lord is the beginning of knowledge." Not fear as in being afraid of God but fear as in respecting his laws and commands. My friend, whenever God instructs or request something from us, it's for our own benefit and to put something into our hands that will not only bless and inspire us but others as well. Many suffer in this life because they have decided to live life on their own terms and conditions. They have foolishly decided to omit God's Word, plans, and intentions. As a result, they and others suffer tremendously.

Your actions affect others either positively or negatively. Everything you say and do has the power to heal or hurt others. Therefore watch what you say and be intentional in what you do, for you will eat the fruit thereof. Life and death is in the power of the tongue. (See Proverbs 18:21.)

To Truly Love Is to Be Totally Free

The purpose for writing this book is to help you understand that to truly love yourself and others is liberating. Luke 10:27 states, "Thou shalt love the Lord thy God with all thy heart, and with all thy soul, and with all thy strength, and with all thy mind; and thy neighbour as thyself." My friend, this fulfills all scripture and allows us to fulfill all the duties of man. Not only that, to love is to have God because God is love.

When you have the love of God, you have an unstoppable force working within you. This force also worked for you. When you have the love of God, my friend, you have everything, and *nothing shall by any means hurt you*. When you have love, no weapon the enemy can form will hurt you. When you have love, all of your needs will be met. When you have love, you're free to love others. When you have love, you can love and appreciate yourself. When you have love, you appreciate the way God has formed you. When you have love, you allow God's perfect will to be accomplished in you and in the earth. When you have love, you allow God to perfect those things and those people around you. When you have love, you have patience, kindness, longsuffering, peace, love, and joy. When you have love, you have freedom. My friend, to repeat what I said already, the love of God comes to set you free, according to John 8:36.

When you have love, you have power and freedom to accomplish any goal you set. You will have the power through the Spirit of God to accomplish any task. You will have the freedom and power to reach your destiny. You will have power to set others free. You will have the power to overcome any issue. You will have power to heal the sick, raise the dead, open blind eyes, and do many miracles because the love of God is cure. The love of God will saturate you, liberate you, accommodate you, translate you, separate you, and communicate with you and for you. The love of God even stops others who might try to frustrate you. The love of God breaks down walls and bulldozes its way through barriers. To have love is to be totally free, totally unstoppable. Now you have God on your side. To fulfill any of this, you need power. Luke 10:19 says, " Behold, I give unto you power to tread on serpents and scorpions, and over all the power of the enemy: and nothing shall by any means hurt you." Why? Because love is cure. There's no force on earth more powerful than love because God is love.

Freely You Give, Freely You Will Receive

We've all heard the term that everything has a price. We know that nothing worthwhile is ever given totally free. But what if I told you that the only cost to love is a loss of pride? Love covers a multitude of faults. That means that you should give away forgiveness to those who may not even be sorry. Give forgiveness to those who might have intentionally or unintentionally wronged you. This is so that you might be set free. Forgiveness is self-liberating. Now I'm not saying that we should allow people to walk all over us. I'm not saying that we should be a doormat. I am not saying to stay in abusive relationships. But what I am saying is to not allow the residue of other people's shortcomings to have a lasting negative effect on you! I'm saying not to allow the negative experiences to remain in your mind, in your heart, and at the forefront of your thoughts. If you hold onto these negative thoughts and emotions, you can even commit suicide. I have listened to neuroscientist Dr. Caroline Leaf, who travels the world explaining how negative thoughts are toxic to our healthy existence. According to Dr. Leaf, every negative thought we have creates black spots on our brains.[17] Now imagine what happens to us when we don't forgive. You allow yourself to file this negative emotion away in your mind because when the file or the memory of that person comes up, this releases a negative chemical and a negative

---

[17] Caroline Leaf, M.D., "Thoughts Have a Viral Effect On Your Mind," *Dr. Leaf's Blog,* June 27, 2011, https://drleaf.com/blog/thoughts-have-a-viral-effect-on-your-mind/.

emotion in your brain, in you.

My friend, what I'm saying here is to do yourself a favor by forgiving. This will set you free from continuing to relive those negative situations. Your mind replays these incidents over and over in your head. It's time for you to liberate yourself and let all those negative thoughts of toxic people go. It's time to free yourself. Understand that, yes, people made serious mistakes, and one thing led to another negative thing. You might think that the person caused you too much pain. You might wonder about all that you endured as a result of this person. Believe me, my friend, I truly understand your pain. I have been there. I know what it's like to live in the land of, "I can't believe you did this to me." I know how it feels to want to scream in frustration. I know what it's like to drink just to cover up the pain. I know what it's like to be let down by those that should have lifted you up. I know what it's like to be betrayed by those whom you were counting on. I know what it's like to be abandoned by those who should have had your back. I know what it's like to be lied to. I know what it's like to have given so much of yourself to others and then turn around and have no one to give to you. I know what it's like to be disappointed. I know what it's like to forgive.

My friend, as I sit here typing this book today, I feel so liberated and so free. No matter how individuals have wronged me, that's on them. I'm free to love. And that alone liberates and empowers me. Their mistakes can no longer hinder me. This feeling is so empowering. It feels so much greater than harboring unforgiveness in my heart and mind. It feels great to consider as nothing what those people have done to me. The negative things that people have done have no effect on me. And because of that, I tell you today that I am free. Free to love again, free to forgive mistakes, and free to understand that people will make mistakes. But now I know that I will not let negativity destroy me. It feels great to be free. I no longer have to drink to feel numb or to cover up the pain. I no longer have to walk around angry at people for not loving me back or for giving me the opposite of what I know I deserve. I am free to love. I have no space in me for those negative emotions. Thank God, I'm free!

Love Heals

Can you see that this is why the enemy has fought you so hard and for so long? His goal was to keep you away from wholly experiencing the true love of God. The enemy understood that, if he could keep you preoccupied long enough, you'd give up, turn back, or remain stagnant, no longer willing to pursue the very thing that God is. And that's love.

Imagine setting a goal of love. In front of the goal is a huge barrier, fighting you off, offending you, calling you names, prohibiting you from moving ahead, insulting you, telling you that you might as well give up because you'll never make this goal. This enemy is so big and fights so hard in this game because he will use anyone and everything, including family to assist him in keeping you away from the love of God.

He knows that if you ever experience the love of God, your life would be totally changed. The love of God will provide you with a peace that surpasses all understanding. This love gives you joy, and Nehemiah 8:10 tells us that the joy of the lord is your strength. With that strength, comes the power to look past the faults of others and see their needs. The enemy knows that God is love. With that love, comes power, a force to be reckoned with.

If God is love and you have love, then you have God, and he is with you. You have everything you'll ever need. That same love of God has the power to heal. I'm a firm believer that the reasons we don't see many manifested healings of God happen in the church today is because of a love deficiency. As the Body of Christ, we don't understand fully that our words, our touch, carry healing.

One day, I had back pain, and a close relative began to rub my back. Instantly, that pain went away. Another day, the same thing happened except this time, my head was hurting. One relative began to massage my head, but nothing happened. When another began to do the same thing, instantly, healing happened again. I noticed that when certain individuals tended to me, the healing was instant. When others touched me who seemed like they really didn't care, their touch didn't have the power to change the condition.

Well Done

"Many will say to me in that day, Lord, Lord, have we not prophesied in thy name? and in thy name have cast out devils? and in thy name done many wonderful works? And then will I profess unto them, I never knew you: depart from me, ye that work iniquity" (Matthew 7:22-23).

The whole goal of a true believer is to make it into the kingdom and to hear the words, "Well done, my good and faithful servant." Not, "depart from me, ye that work iniquity." But what exactly is iniquity? Webster's defines iniquity as: 1. gross injustice : wickedness 2. a wicked act or thing: sin.[18] Another definition of the word is immoral or grossly unfair behavior.[19] Additional synonyms include wickedness, sinfulness, immorality, impropriety.[20]

Now let's define wickedness because sometimes we see words and don't have the slightest idea as to the deeper meaning they possess. And therefore, we might not take things seriously or continue to walk in error. It's easy to walk in error simply because we have no idea that we are being ignorant. The Bible says in Hosea 4:6, "My people are destroyed for lack of knowledge." Sometimes we might not know that we are walking in error because we lack knowledge of what error is. So, let's define and dig deeper into the word *wickedness*. Wickedness is defined as the quality of being evil or morally wrong. [21]

The whole idea of this story is to be aware of the fact that God's love is cure, not only for you but for the entire world around you. God's love heals, restores, justifies, and forgives. His love and the love that we share sustains us and others. His love abounds toward us more and more. With his love, relationships are restored. That's why we cannot afford to live our lives without the love of God. I mentioned what my dad said to me during a phone call. He told me that he didn't love himself, and he didn't know what love was. That's primarily because he lacked a relationship with God that provided him with the power to love. Without a relationship with God, you will not have the power to love others in a healthy way nor will you have the ability to maintain that love. God's love is intentional because he knows that love is power. It restores us. His love brings healing to our spirit, mind, and body. And without it, we'd curl up and die. We were made for love. The enemy's goal is to overwhelm and frustrate you, to tire you out so that you give up on others, on life, and on love. He knows that God is love, and without

---

[18] *Merriam-Webster*, "iniquity (*n.*)," accessed February 25, 2018,
https://www.merriam-webster.com/dictionary/iniquity.
[19] *Oxford Dictionary*, "iniquity (*n.*)," accessed February 25, 2018,
https://en.oxforddictionaries.com/definition/iniquity.
[20] *Oxford Dictionary (Thesaurus)*, "iniquity (*n.*)," accessed February 25, 2018.
https://en.oxforddictionaries.com/thesaurus/iniquity.
[21] *Oxford Dictionary*, "wickedness (*n.*)," accessed February 25, 2018,
https://en.oxforddictionaries.com/definition/wickedness.

God, you can do nothing. But with God, who is love, then all things become possible for you, your family, community, and the world.

Closing Prayer

Father God, In the name of Jesus, we enter into your gates and into your courts with praise and thanksgiving. Thank you that no weapon that is formed against us shall prosper. We thank you for every gift you have given us. We now know and understand that our children and everything that we own are gifts from you. Father, we ask that you forgive us of all our sins. We confess that Jesus Christ is the Son of God and that he died on the cross for us. On the third day, he rose again with all power in his hands.

I thank you for your Son because he died so that we might live. I thank you that because Jesus lives, I can face tomorrow. I understand that, according to Isaiah 53, he was wounded for our transgressions; he was bruised for our iniquity; the chastisement of our peace was upon him, and by his stripes we were healed.

I thank God that I am healed today. I claim my healing by faith. I release all hurt, bitterness, anger, strife, and every disappointment in my life over to you. I forgive all who have sinned against me. I release them, and I also release myself. I refuse to be bound to hurt bitterness, fear, disappointment, and strife.

I thank you, Lord, for giving me the power to cast my cares upon you because you care for me. I now know that I don't need to carry this burden any longer, for on this day, I let go of everything that blocks your love from flowing in my life. I know that in Mark 12:30-31, you gave the commandment to love the Lord your God with all your heart, all of your soul, and with everything that is within me, and to love my neighbor as yourself.

Father, forgive me if I have not loved well. Forgive me for when I have not walked in love. I decree and declare now that my love shall not be stolen by the enemy and that you have always given me a grace to love. I want the *agape* kind of love. I now know that love will cover a multitude of faults—my own and others. From this day forward, I refuse to allow the enemy to rob me of the right to love. I ask that you bless my family and bless those who have hurt me.

Bless my future and heal me of my past. Restore unto me now the years that the cankerworm, the palmerworm, and the caterpillar have eaten up. (See Joel 2:25.) In Jesus's name I pray,

Amen.

About the Author

Defying all odds, Talicia Parker overcame a dysfunctional and abusive childhood to become a true leader and catalyst for change. Although she dropped out of high school, she has since obtained her GED and has taken college classes. She worked for Fortune 500 insurance companies where she dominated her field, leading record-breaking sales teams and serving as a sales coach and staff motivator. In 1999, Talicia launched her first two businesses: Tee-Tee's Hot Dogs and Daedell's Barber Studio. She remained in business for five years until God called her into ministry.

Talicia has received certifications in Christian counseling, psychology, and evangelism. She has a background in governmental markets, management, and leadership training and development. She has attended numerous ministry classes and is licensed as a minister by Dr. Bill Winston. She also completed formal certification with John Maxwell as a professional coach, teacher, trainer, and speaker.

Reaching beyond the pulpit into the community to empower and transform others, Talicia is also the founder and CEO of the House of Issachar Community Development Corporation. This strategic re-entry program is designed to strengthen the lives of under-resourced men, women, and children, providing them with hope for the future.

www.ingramcontent.com/pod-product-compliance
Lightning Source LLC
Chambersburg PA
CBHW031557040426
42452CB00006B/332